For Engineers & Designers

IRONCAD Exercises

200 3D PRACTICE DRAWINGS

SACHIDANAND JHA

Dear Reader,

Thank you for choosing **IRONCAD Exercises** book. This book is part of a family of premium-quality CADIN360 books, all of which are written by Outstanding author who combine practical experience with a gift for teaching.

CADIN360 was founded in 2016. More than 3 years later, we're still committed to producing consistently exceptional books. With each of our titles, we're working hard to set a new standard for the industry. From the paper we print on, to the authors we work with, our goal is to bring you the best books available.

I hope you see all that reflected in these pages. I'd be very interested to hear your comments and get your feedback on how we're doing. Feel free to let me know what you think about this or any other CADIN360 book by sending me an email at contactus@cadin360.com.

If you think you've found a technical error in this book, please visit
https://cadin360.com/contact-us/.
Customer feedback is critical to our efforts at CADIN360.

Best regards,

Sachidanand Jha
Founder & CEO, CADIN360

IRONCAD Exercises

Published by
CADIN360
cadin360.com

Limit of Liability/Disclaimer of Warranty:

Examination Copies

Electronic Files

Disclaimer:

Preface

IRONCAD Exercises

❖ This book contain 200 CAD practice exercises and drawings.

❖ This book does not provide step by step tutorial to design 3D models.

❖ S.I Unit is used.

❖ Predominantly used Third Angle Projection.

❖ This book is for **IRONCAD** and Other Feature-Based Modeling Software such as Inventor, SolidWorks, NX, Solid Edge, AutoCAD, PTC Creo etc.

❖ It is intended to provide Drafters, Designers and Engineers with enough 3D CAD exercises for practice on **IRONCAD**.

❖ It includes almost all types of exercises that are necessary to provide, clear, concise and systematic information required on industrial machine part drawings.

❖ Third Angle Projection is intentionally used to familiarize Drafters, Designers and Engineers in Third Angle Projection to meet the expectation of world wide Engineering drawing print.

❖ Clear and well drafted drawing help easy understanding of the design.

❖ This book is for Beginner, Intermediate and Advance CAD users.

❖ These exercises are from Basics to Advance level.

❖ Each exercises can be assigned and designed separately.

❖ No Exercise is a prerequisite for another. All dimensions are in mm.

❖ Note: Assume any missing dimensions.

EX-01

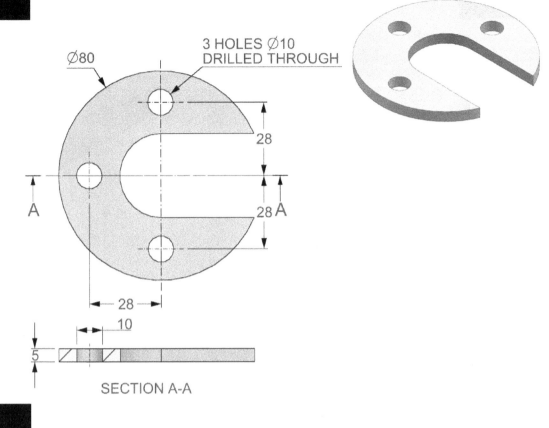

Ø80

3 HOLES Ø10
DRILLED THROUGH

28

28 A

A

28

10

5

SECTION A-A

EX-02

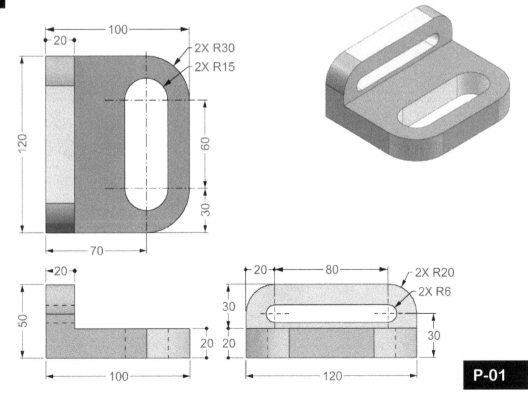

100

20

2X R30

2X R15

120

60

30

70

20

50

20

100

20

80

2X R20

2X R6

30

20

30

120

P-01

EX-03

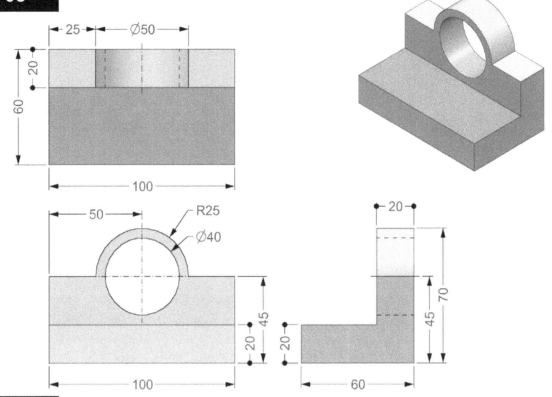

25	Ø50

20
60
100

50 — R25
Ø40
100
45
20

20
70
45
20
60

EX-04

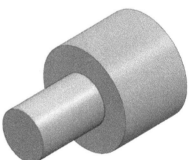

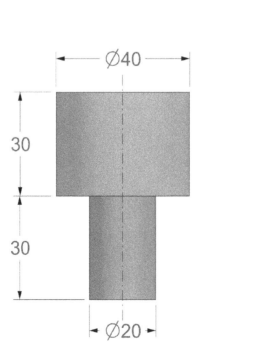

Ø40
30
30
Ø20

P-02

EX-05

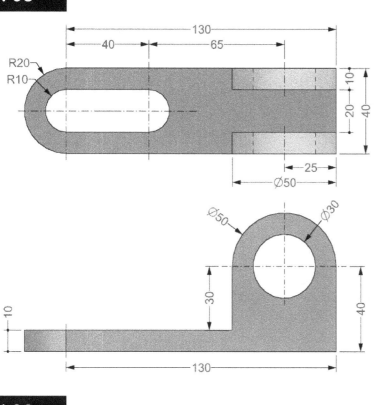

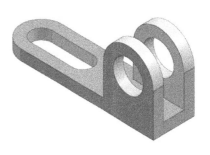

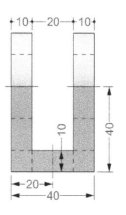

EX-06

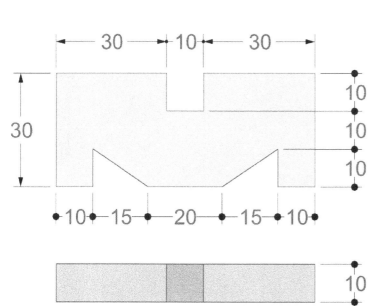

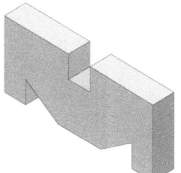

P-03

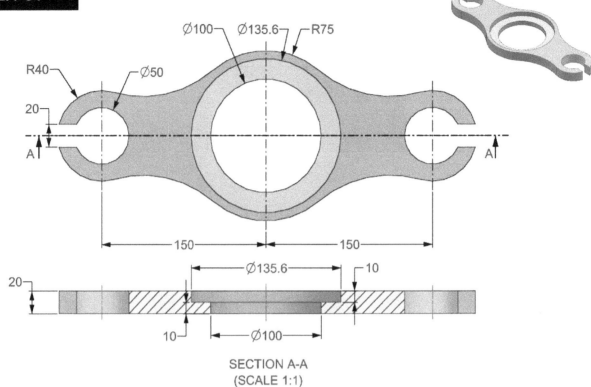

Ø100 Ø135.6 R75

R40 Ø50

20

A

150 150

Ø135.6 10

20

10 Ø100

SECTION A-A
(SCALE 1:1)

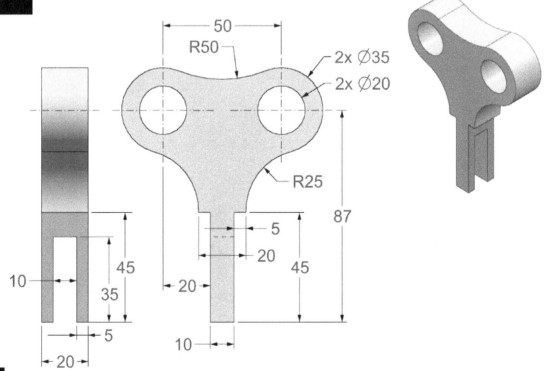

50

R50 2x Ø35

2x Ø20

R25

87

5

20

45

45

10

20

10

45

35

5

20

EX-09

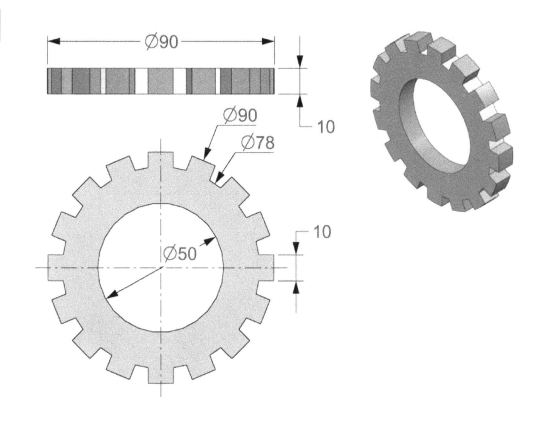

Ø90

10

Ø90
Ø78
Ø50
10

EX-10

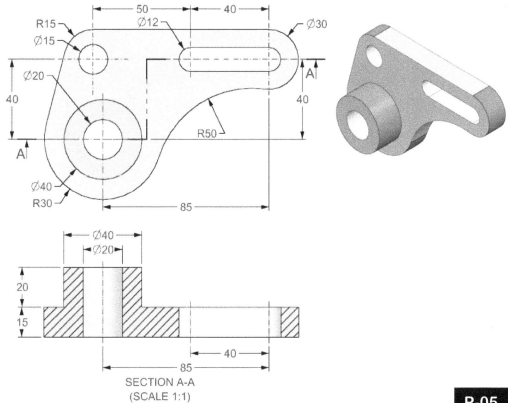

R15
Ø15
Ø12
Ø30
50
40
Ø20
40
40
R50
Ø40
R30
85

Ø40
Ø20
20
15
40
85

SECTION A-A
(SCALE 1:1)

EX-11

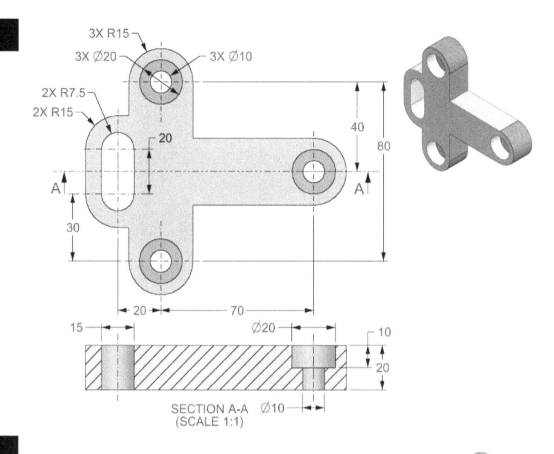

3X R15
3X Ø20
3X Ø10
2X R7.5
2X R15
20
40
80
A
30
20
70
15
Ø20
10
20
SECTION A-A
(SCALE 1:1)
Ø10

EX-12

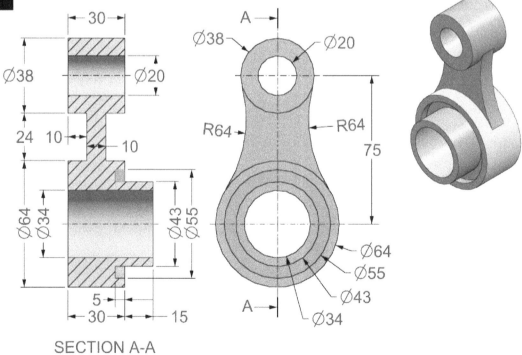

30
Ø38
Ø20
24
10
10
Ø64
Ø34
Ø43
Ø55
5
30
15

SECTION A-A
(SCALE 1:1)

A
Ø38
Ø20
R64
R64
75
Ø64
Ø55
Ø43
Ø34
A

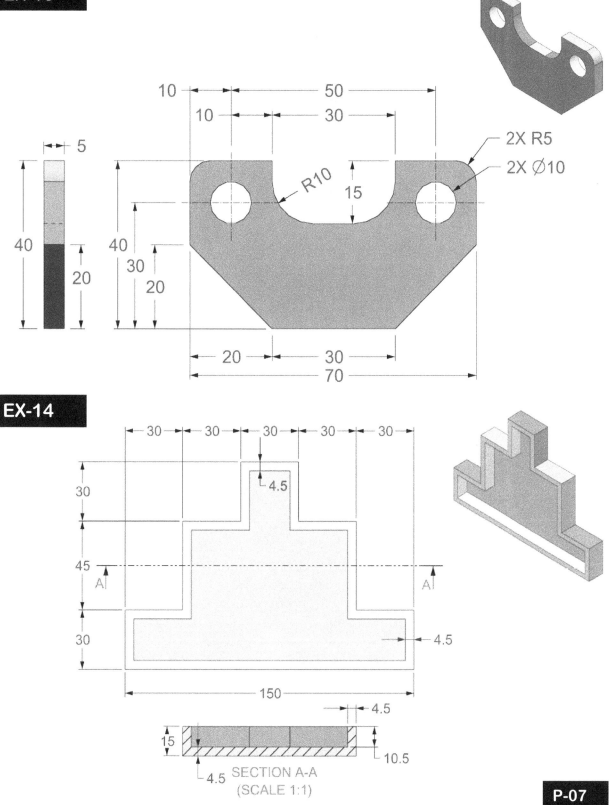

EX-13

10 50
10 30

2X R5
2X Ø10

R10
15

5
40
40 20
30
20

20 30
70

EX-14

30 30 30 30 30

30

4.5

45

A A

30

4.5

150

4.5

15

10.5

4.5 SECTION A-A
(SCALE 1:1)

P-07

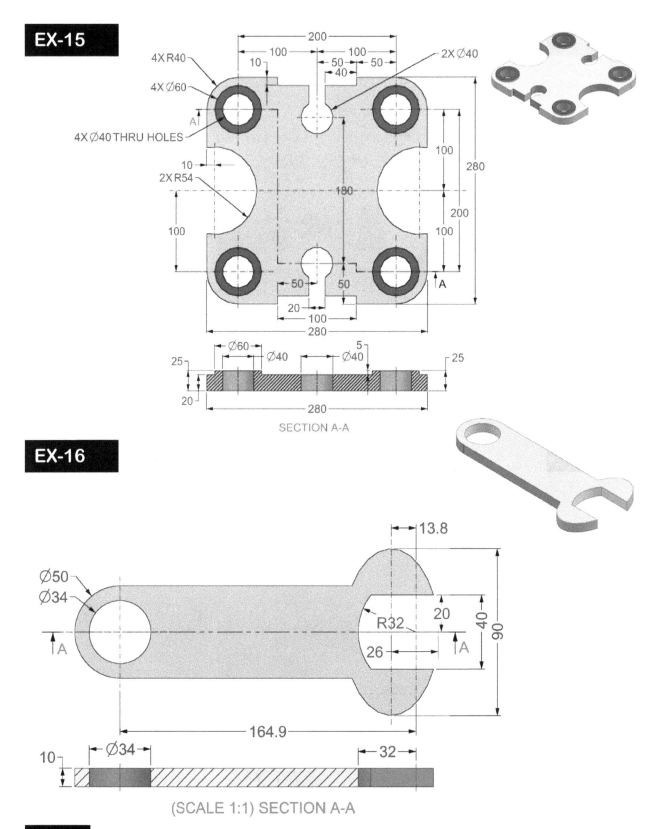

EX-15

4X R40
4X ⌀60
4X ⌀40 THRU HOLES
2X ⌀40
200
100
100
50
50
40
10
A
100
280
100
200
100
2X R54
10
180
100
50
50
20
100
280

⌀60
⌀40
5
⌀40
25
25
20
280

SECTION A-A

EX-16

⌀50
⌀34
13.8
20
40
90
R32
26
A
A
164.9
10
⌀34
32

(SCALE 1:1) SECTION A-A

P-08

EX-17

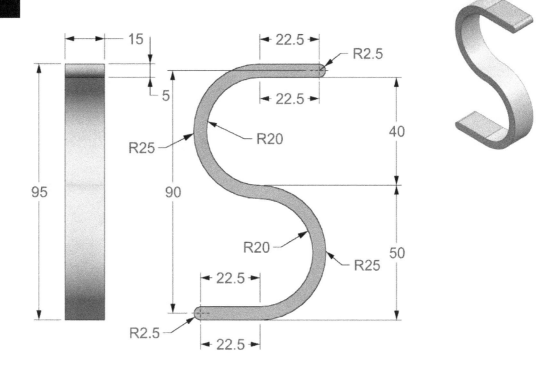

EX-18

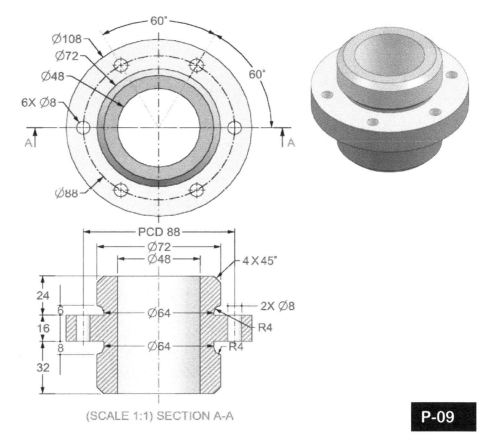

(SCALE 1:1) SECTION A-A

P-09

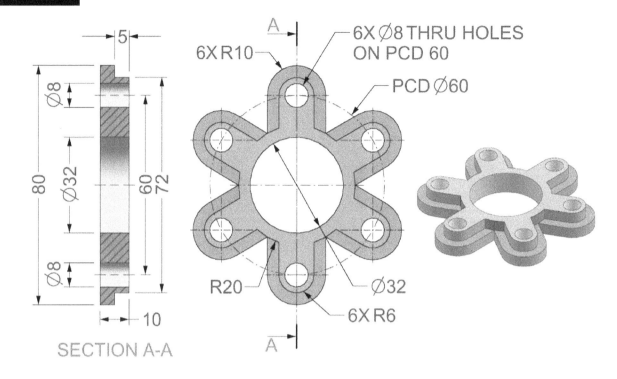

6X R10

6X Ø8 THRU HOLES
ON PCD 60

PCD Ø60

5

Ø8

Ø32

80

60

72

10

R20

Ø32

6X R6

SECTION A-A

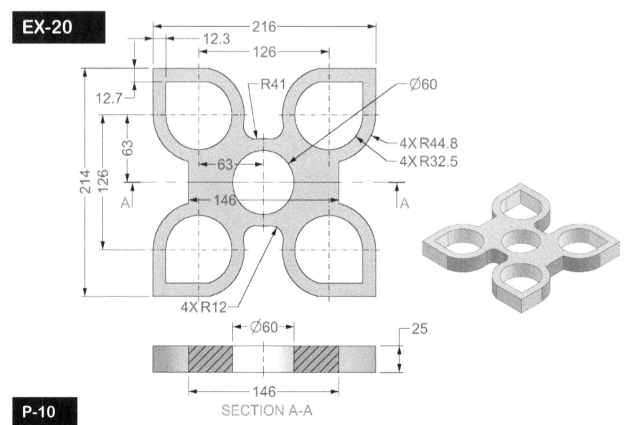

216

12.3

126

12.7

R41

Ø60

4X R44.8
4X R32.5

63

63

214

126

146

4X R12

Ø60

25

146

SECTION A-A

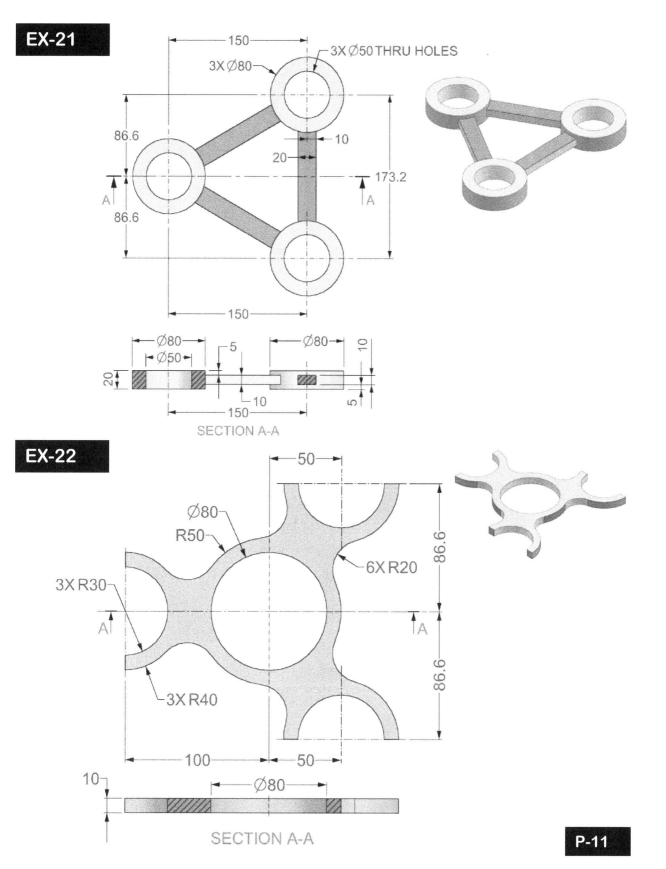

EX-21

150

3X Ø50 THRU HOLES

3X Ø80

86.6

10

20

173.2

A

A

86.6

150

Ø80

Ø50

5

Ø80

10

20

10

5

150

SECTION A-A

EX-22

50

Ø80

R50

86.6

6X R20

3X R30

A

A

86.6

3X R40

100

50

10

Ø80

SECTION A-A

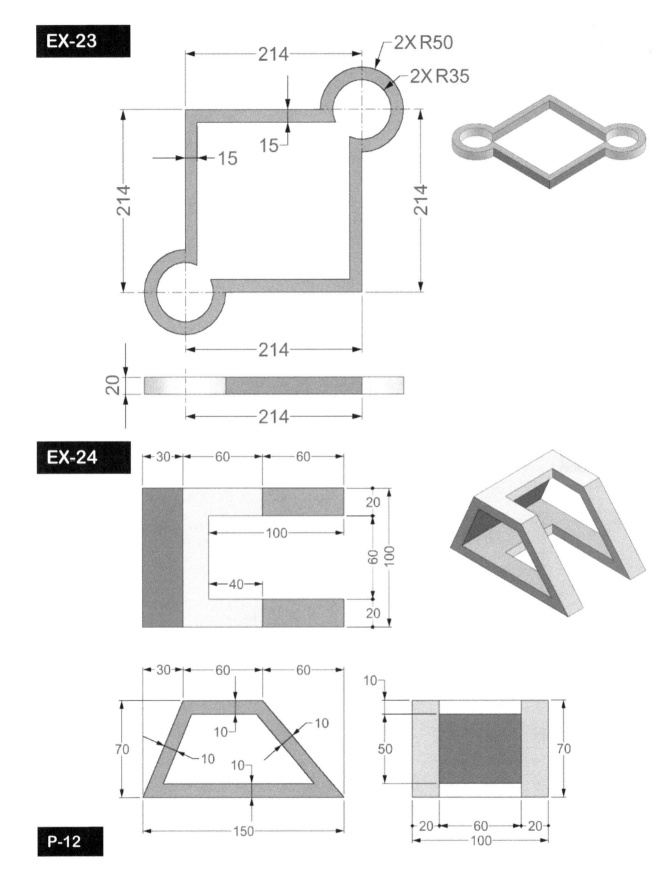

EX-23

214

2X R50

2X R35

15

15

214

214

214

20

214

EX-24

30 60 60

20

100

60 100

40

20

P-12

30 60 60

10

10 10

70

10 10

150

10

50

70

20 60 20

100

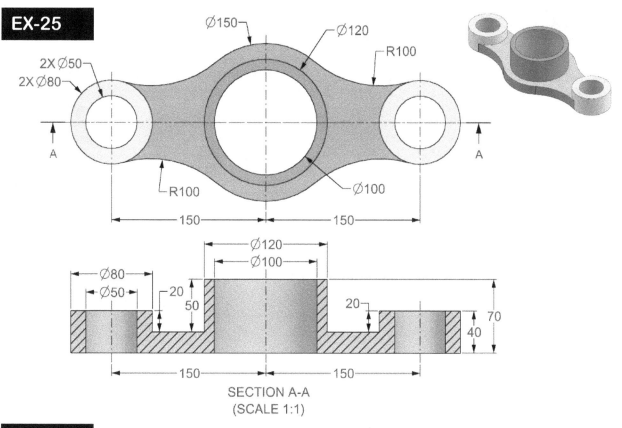

Ø150
Ø120
R100
2X Ø50
2X Ø80
R100
Ø100
150
150

Ø120
Ø100
Ø80
Ø50
20
50
20
70
40
150
150

SECTION A-A
(SCALE 1:1)

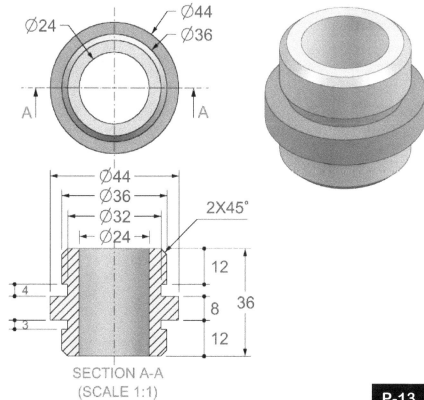

Ø44
Ø24
Ø36

A   A

Ø44
Ø36
Ø32
Ø24
2X45°
12
4
8   36
3
12

SECTION A-A
(SCALE 1:1)

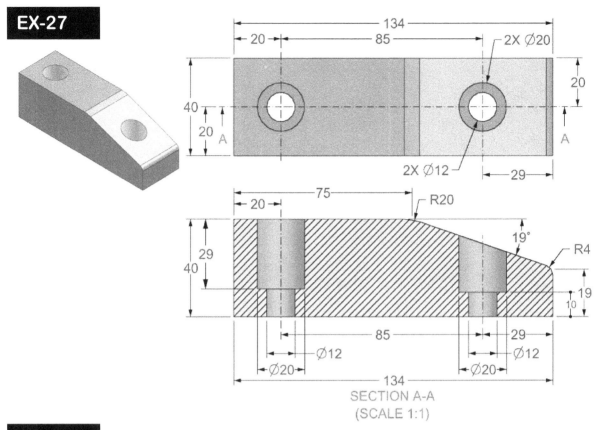

SECTION A-A
(SCALE 1:1)

EX-28

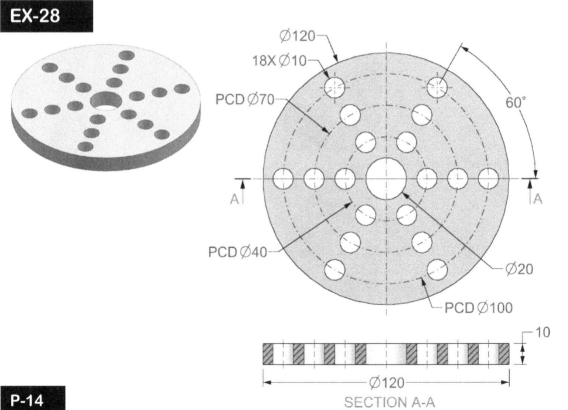

SECTION A-A

EX-29

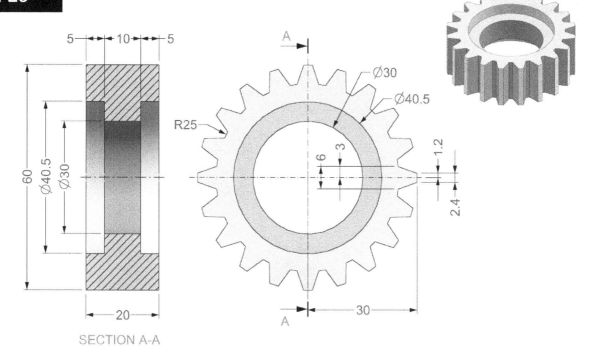

SECTION A-A

EX-30

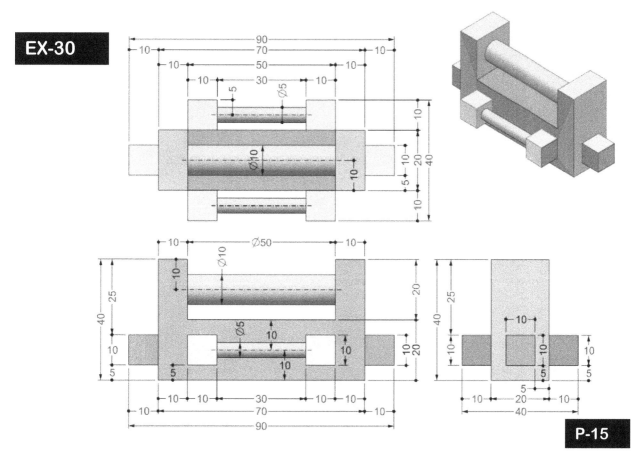

P-15

EX-31

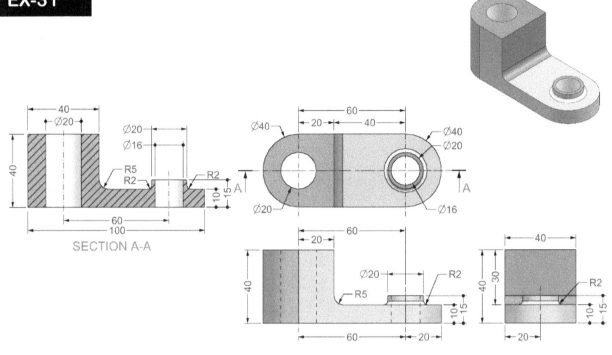

SECTION A-A

EX-32

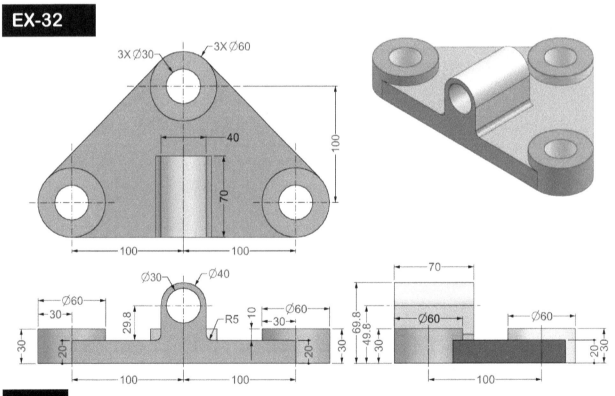

P-16

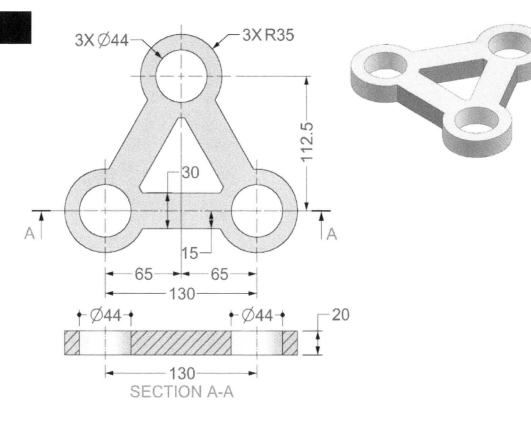

3X Ø44   3X R35

112.5

30

15

65   65

130

Ø44   Ø44   20

130

SECTION A-A

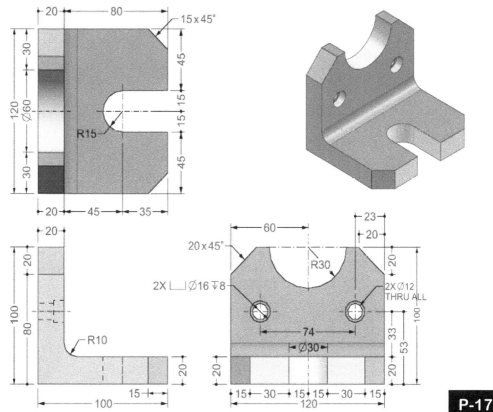

20   80   15 x 45°

30

45

Ø60   15 15

15

R15   15

30   45

20   45   35

20

20   20

100

80

R10

15

100

23

60   20

20 x 45°   R30

20

2X ⌴ Ø16 ↧8   2X Ø12 THRU ALL

74   100

Ø30   33

53

20

15   30   15   15   30   15   20

120

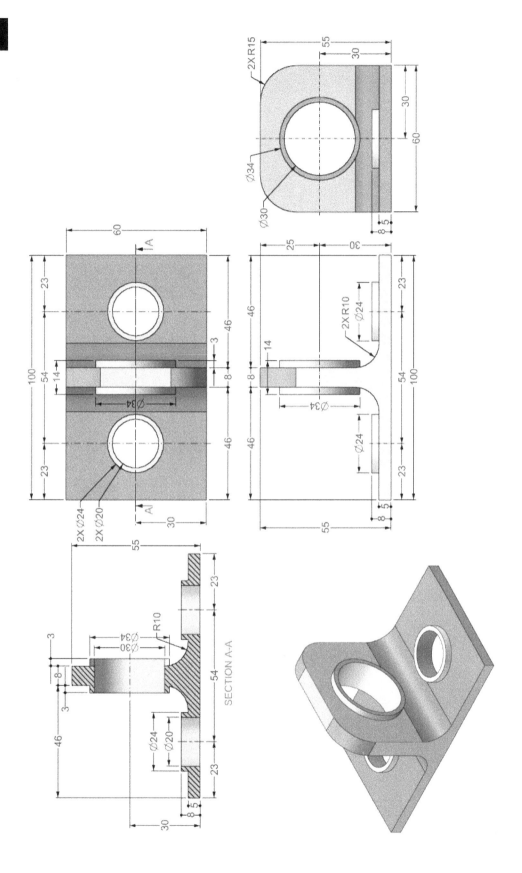

SECTION A-A

EX-36

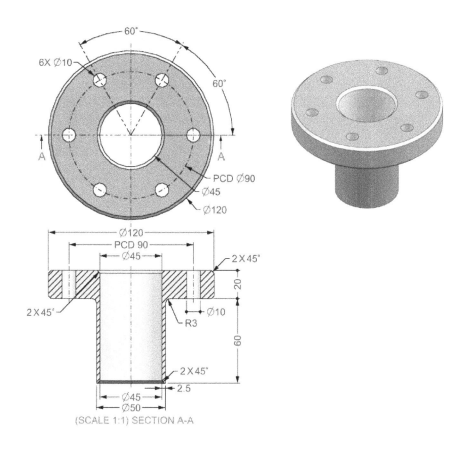

60°
6X Ø10
60°
A
A
PCD Ø90
Ø45
Ø120

Ø120
PCD 90
Ø45
2 X 45°
20
2 X 45°
Ø10
R3
60
2 X 45°
2.5
Ø45
Ø50
(SCALE 1:1) SECTION A-A

EX-37

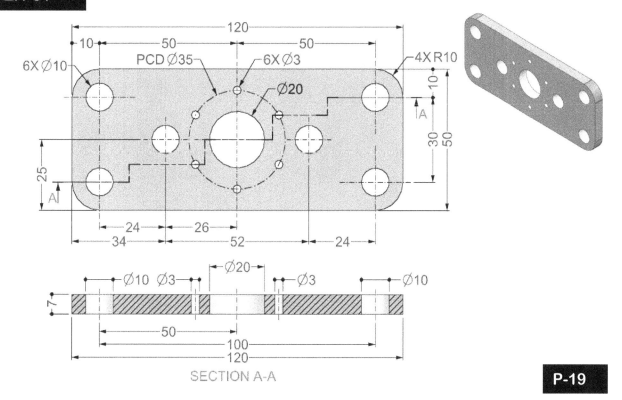

120
10
50
50
6X Ø10
PCD Ø35
6X Ø3
4X R10
Ø20
10
A
30
50
25
A
24
26
34
52
24

Ø20
Ø10   Ø3
Ø3
Ø10
7
50
100
120
SECTION A-A

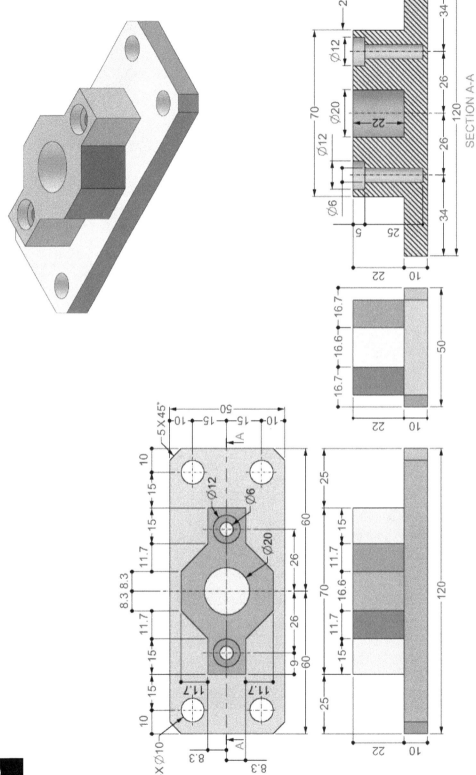

SECTION A-A

EX-39

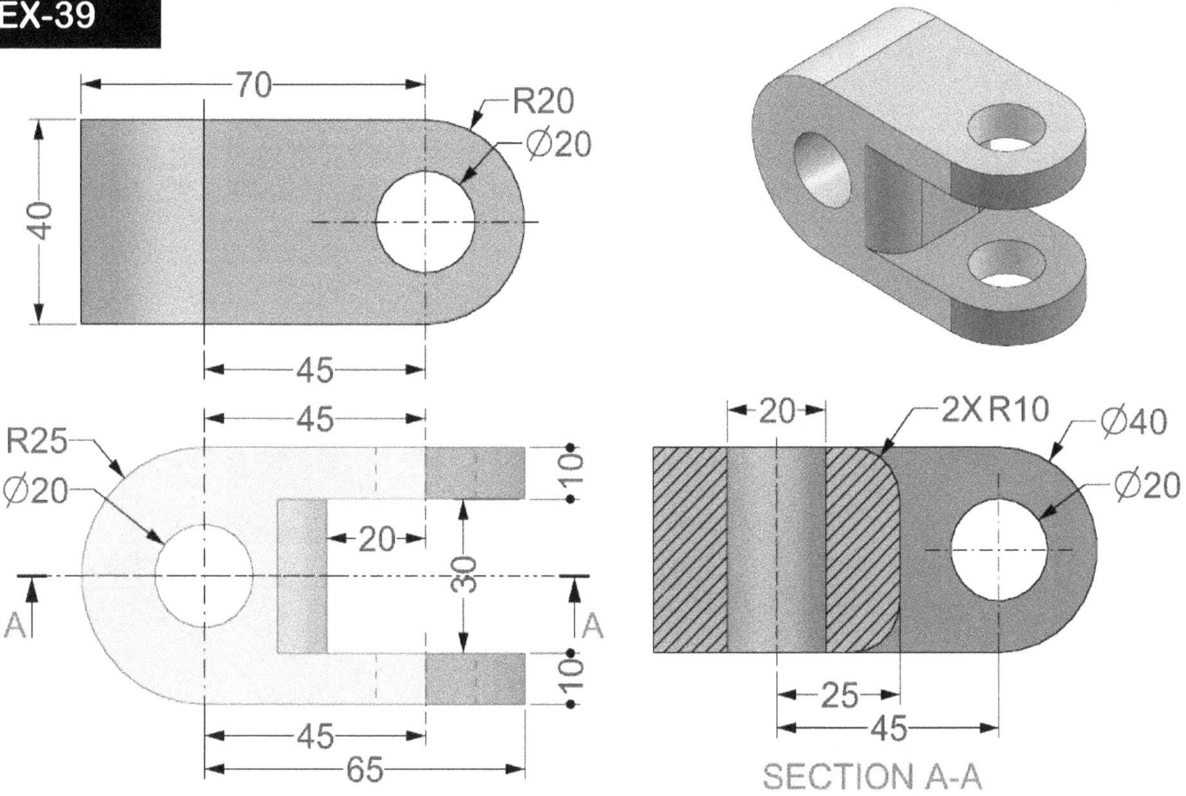

70

R20
Ø20

40

45

R25
Ø20

45

20

30

10

10

A

A

45

65

20

2X R10

Ø40

Ø20

25

45

SECTION A-A

EX-40

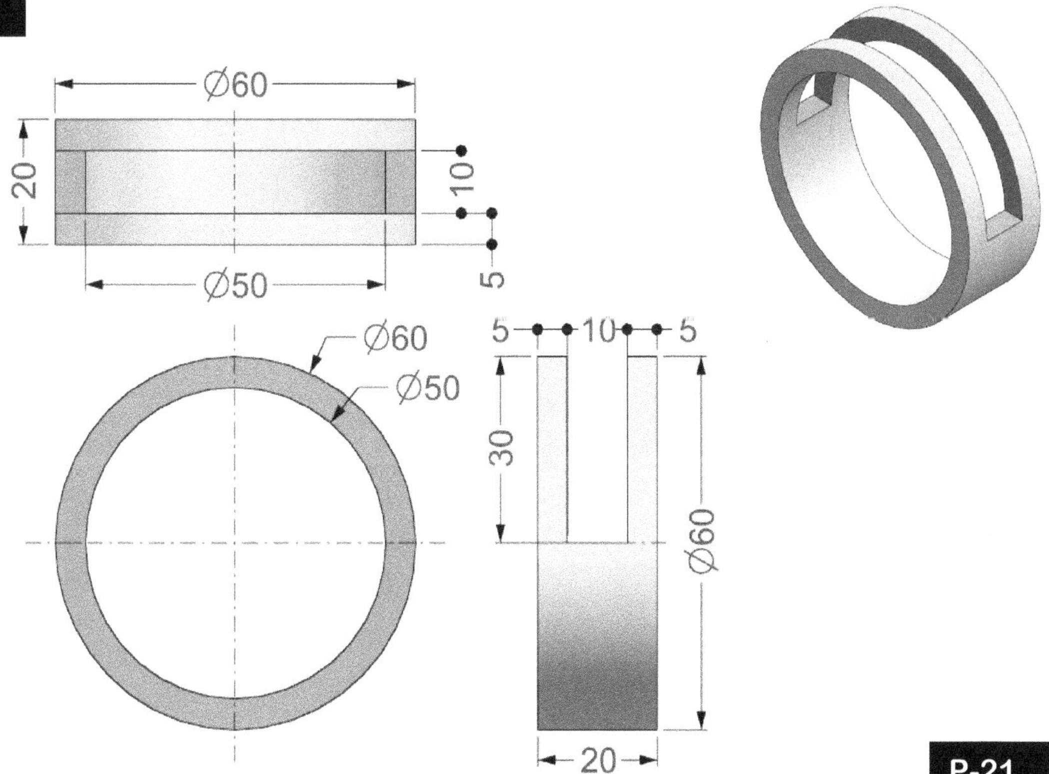

Ø60

20

10

5

Ø50

Ø60
Ø50

5

10

5

30

Ø60

20

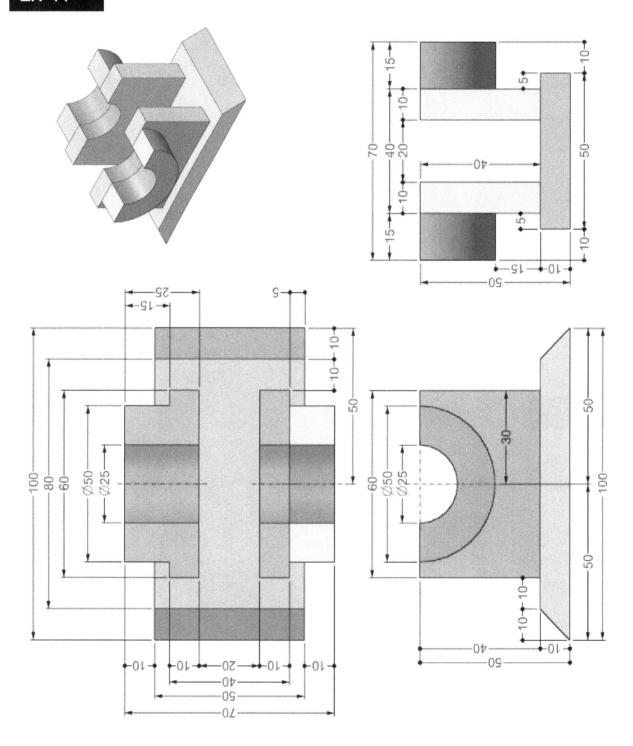

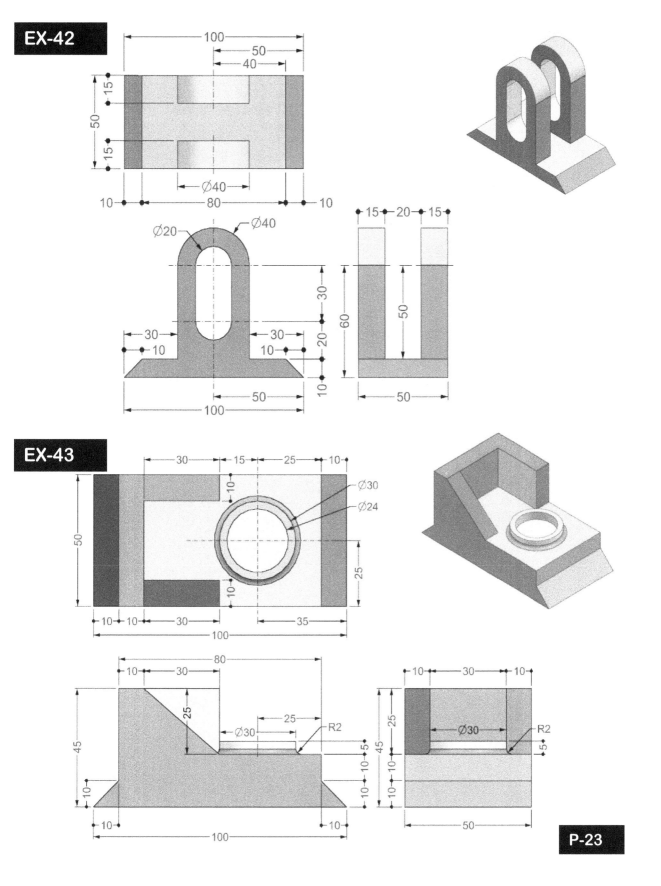

EX-42

EX-43

P-23

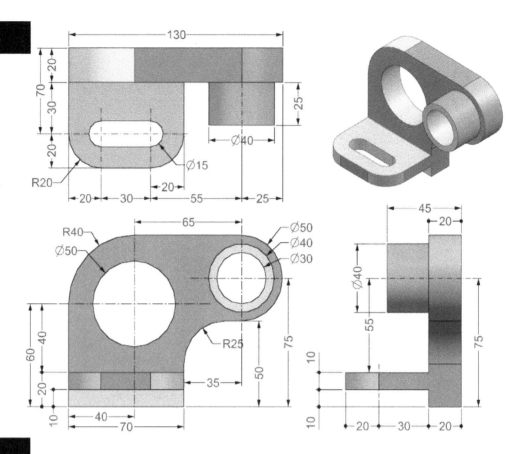

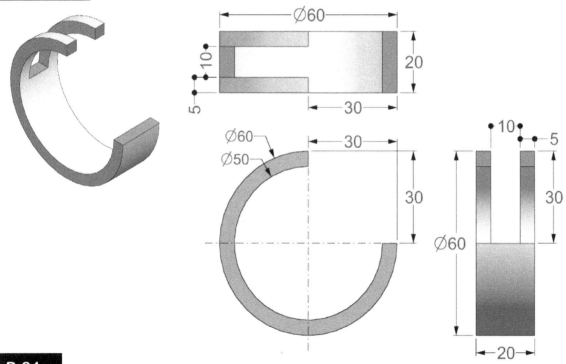

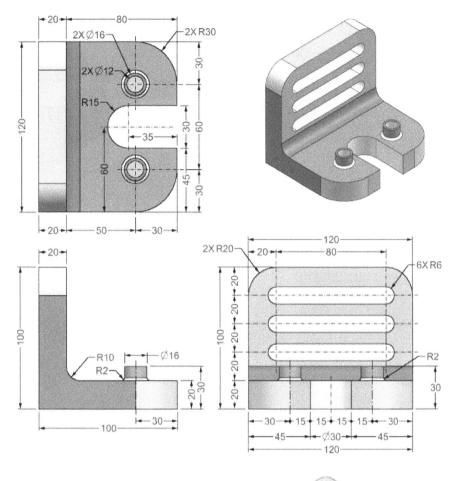

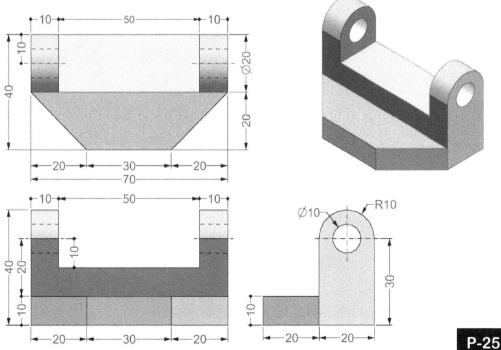

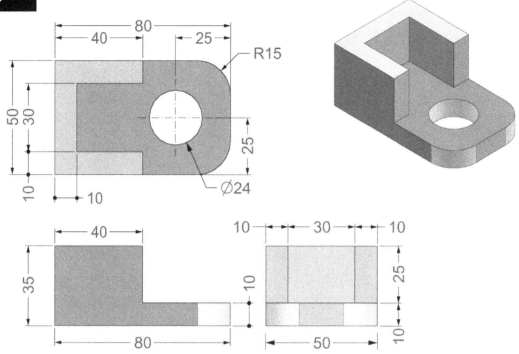

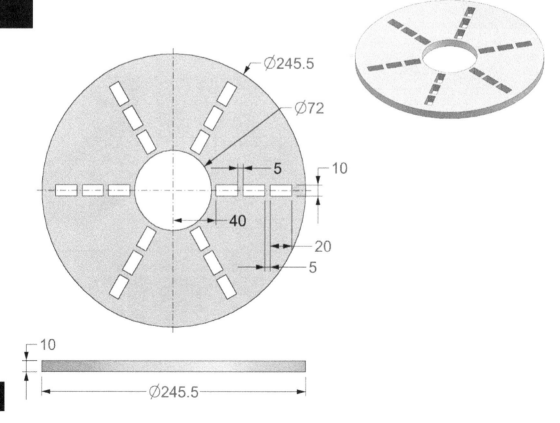

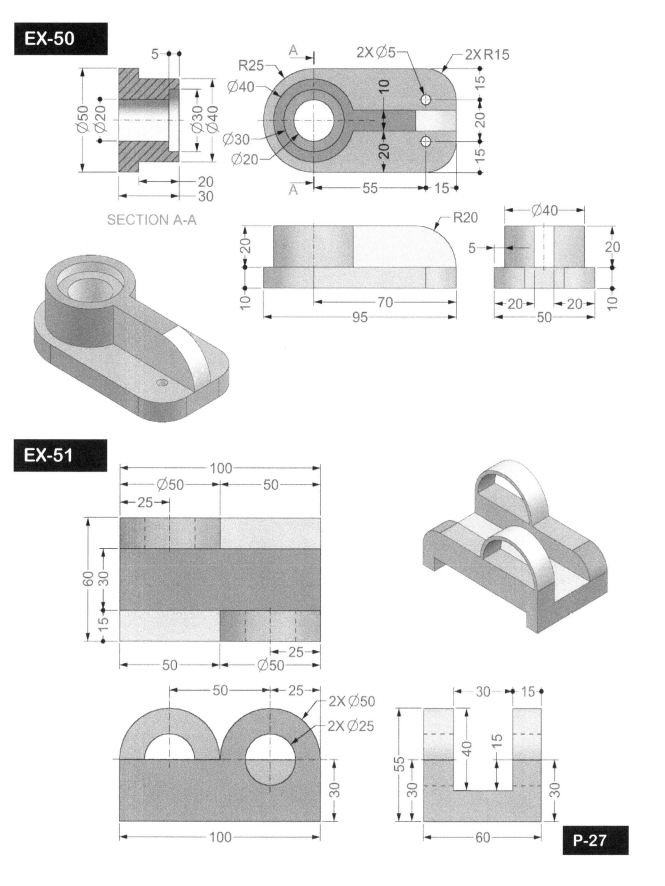

EX-50

5
∅50
∅20
∅30
∅40
20
30

SECTION A-A

A
R25
∅40
∅30
∅20
2X∅5
2XR15
10
15
20
15
20
55
15

R20
20
10
70
95

∅40
5
20
20
20
50
10

EX-51

100
∅50
50
25
60
30
15
50
∅50
25

2X∅50
2X∅25
50
25
30
100

30
15
55
40
15
30
30
60

P-27

EX-52

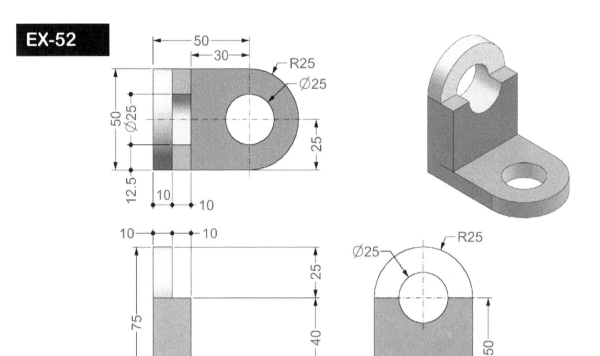

EX-53

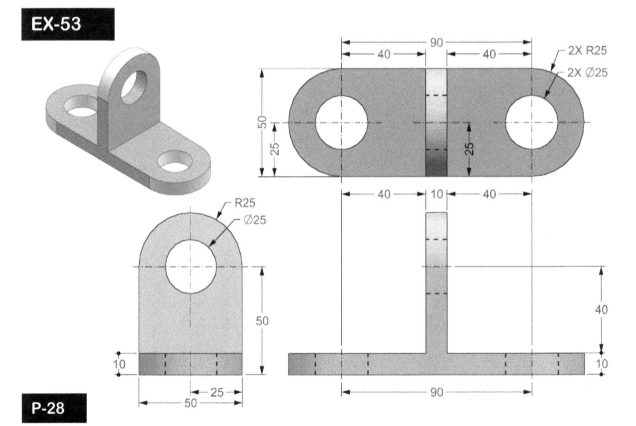

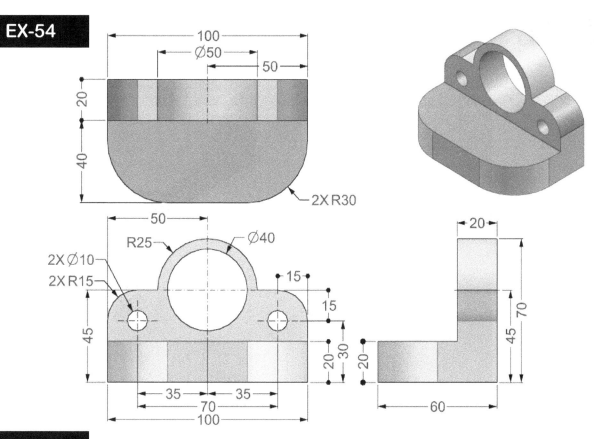

100
Ø50
50
20
40
2X R30

50
R25
Ø40
2X Ø10
2X R15
45
15
15
20
30
20
35
35
70
100

20
70
45
20
60

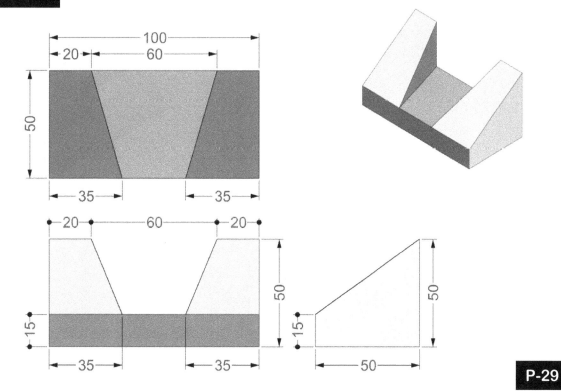

100
20
60
50
35
35

20
60
20
50
15
35
35

50
15
50

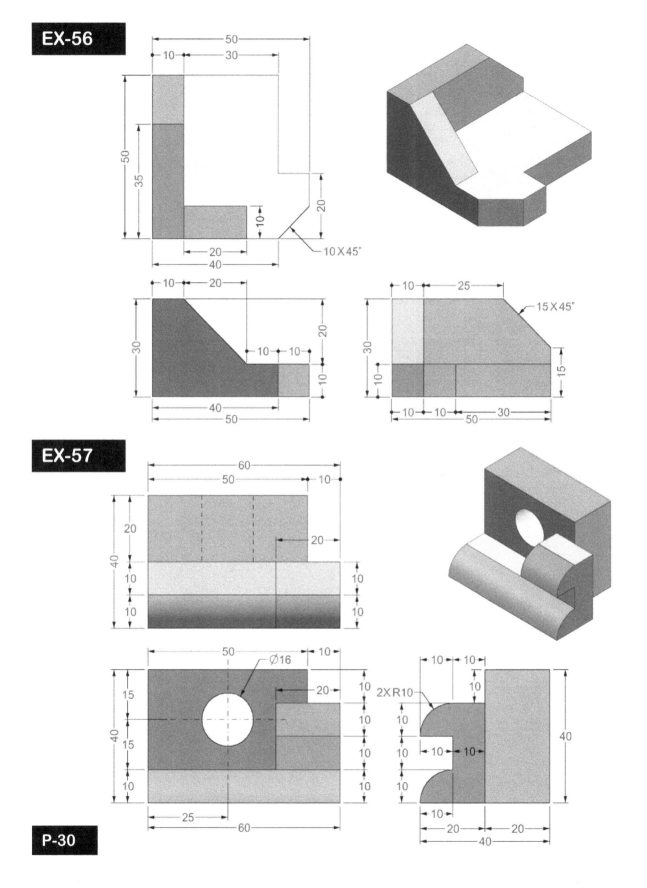

EX-56

EX-57

P-30

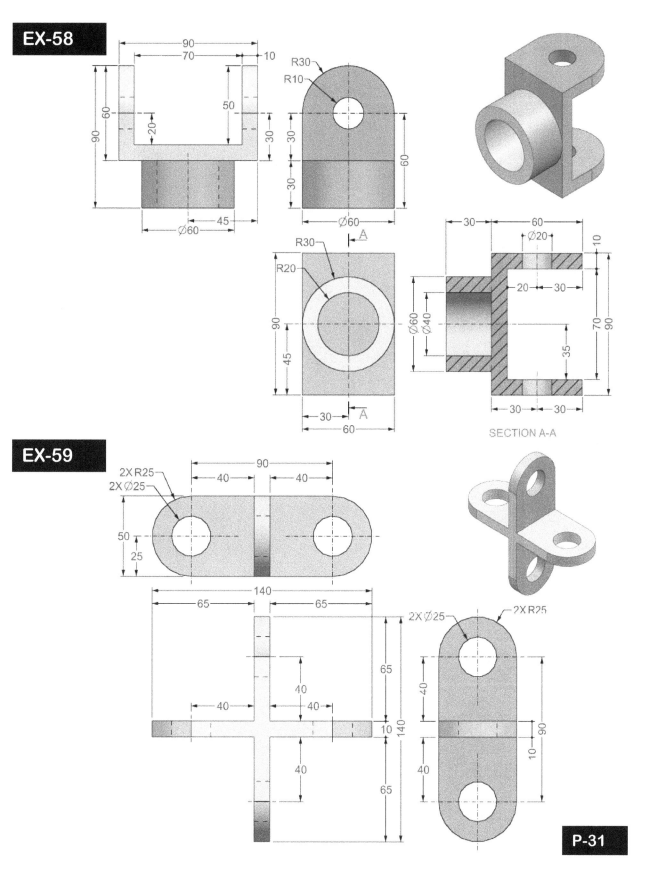

EX-58

R30
R10
90
60
20
90
70
10
50
30
30
45
Ø60

R30
R10
30
30
60
Ø60
A

R30
R20
90
45
30
60
A

30
60
Ø20
10
20
30
Ø60
Ø40
70
90
35
30
30
SECTION A-A

EX-59

2X R25
2X Ø25
90
40
40
50
25

140
65
65
65
40
40
40
10
140
40
40
40
65

2X Ø25
2X R25
40
90
10
40

P-31

EX-60

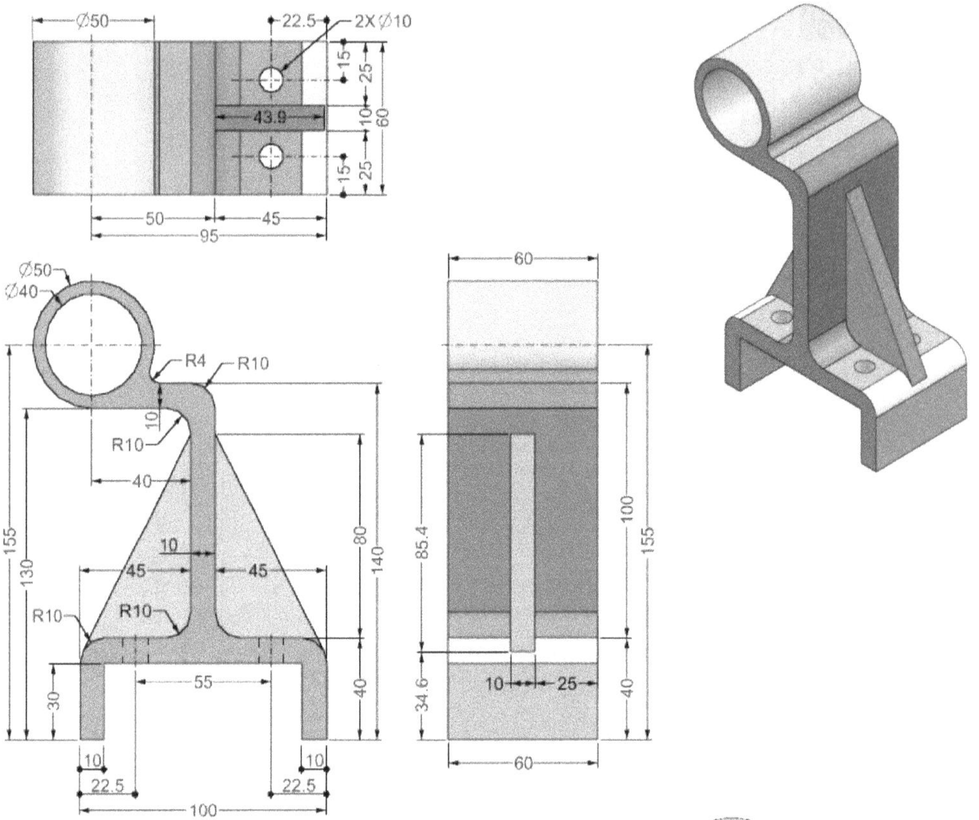

EX-61

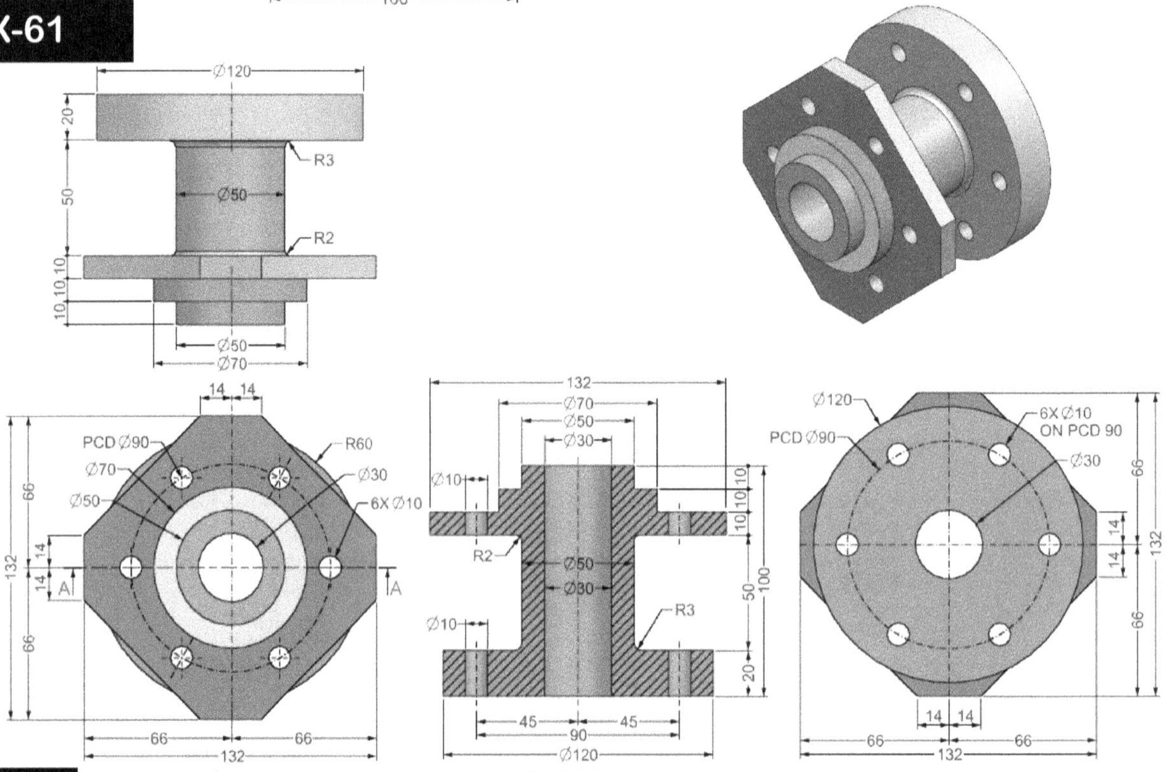

P-32

SECTION A-A

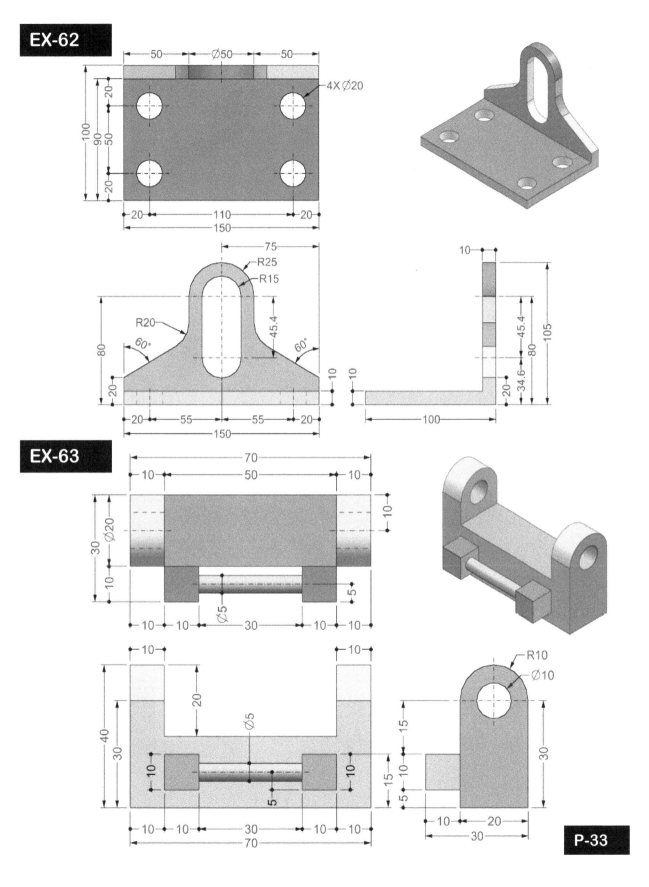

EX-62

EX-63

P-33

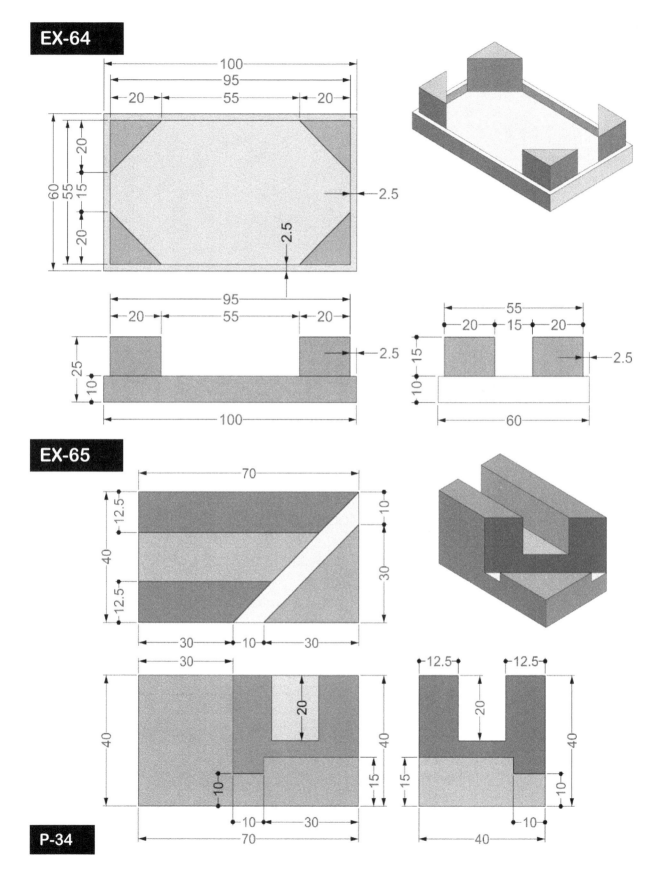

EX-64

EX-65

P-34

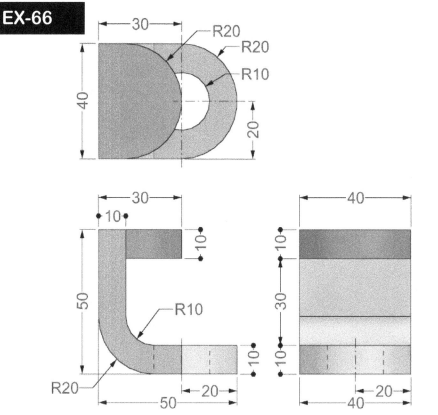

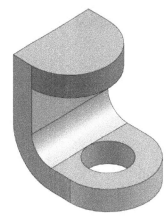

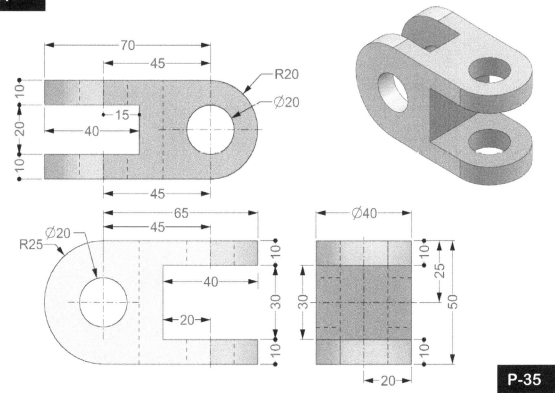

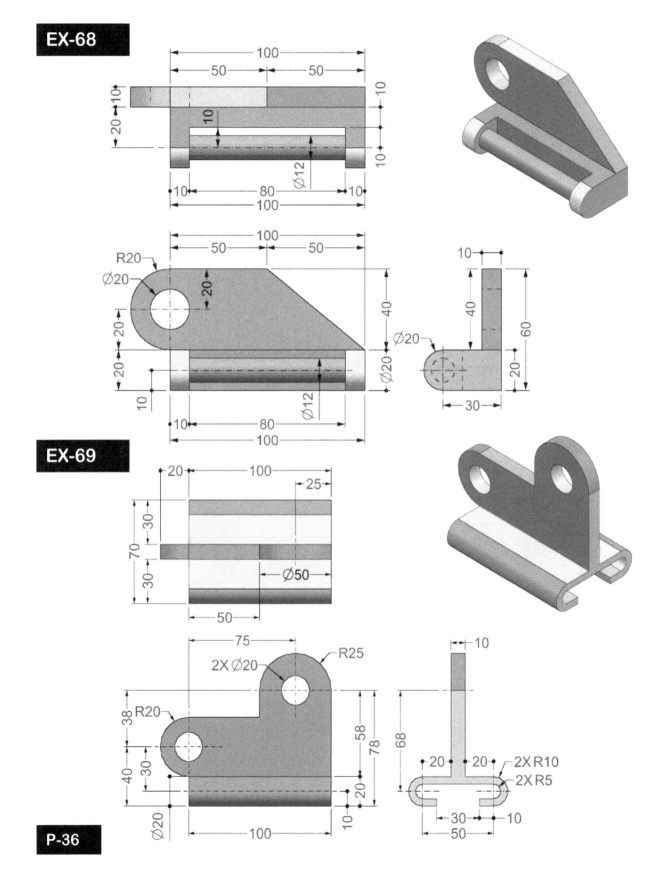

EX-68

EX-69

P-36

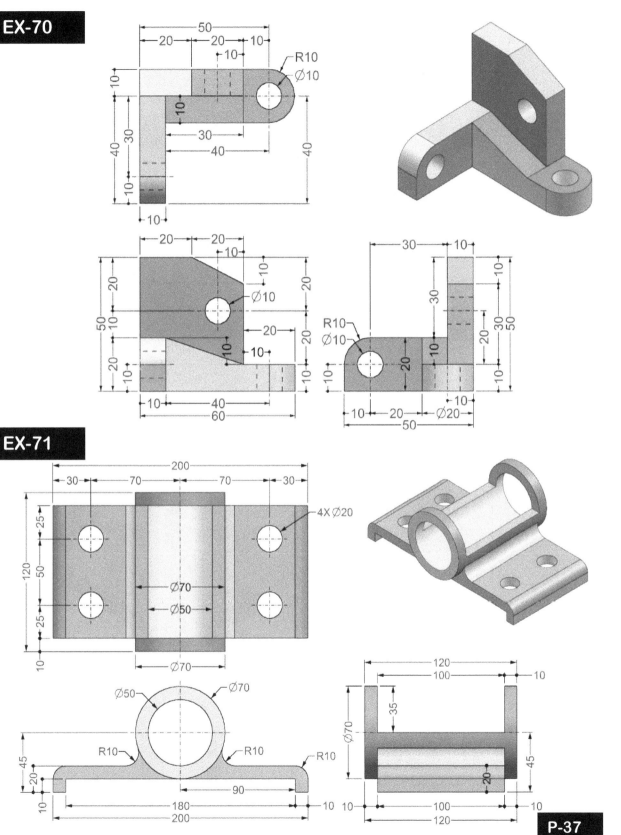

EX-70

EX-71

P-37

EX-72

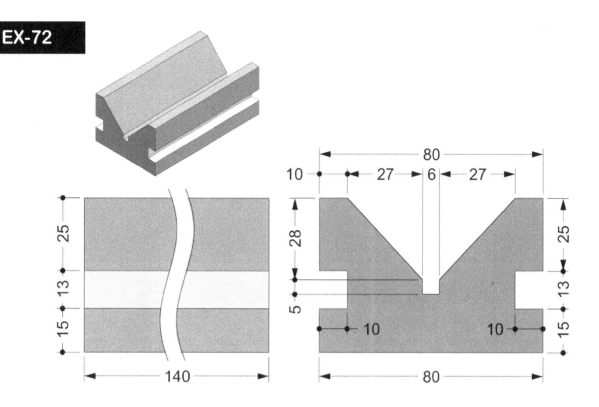

EX-73

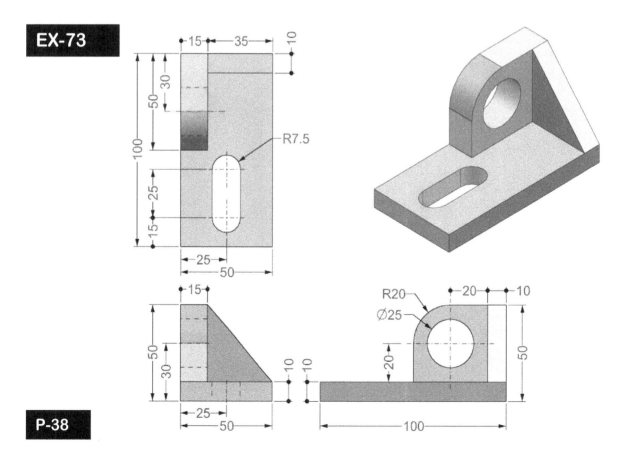

EX-74

EX-75

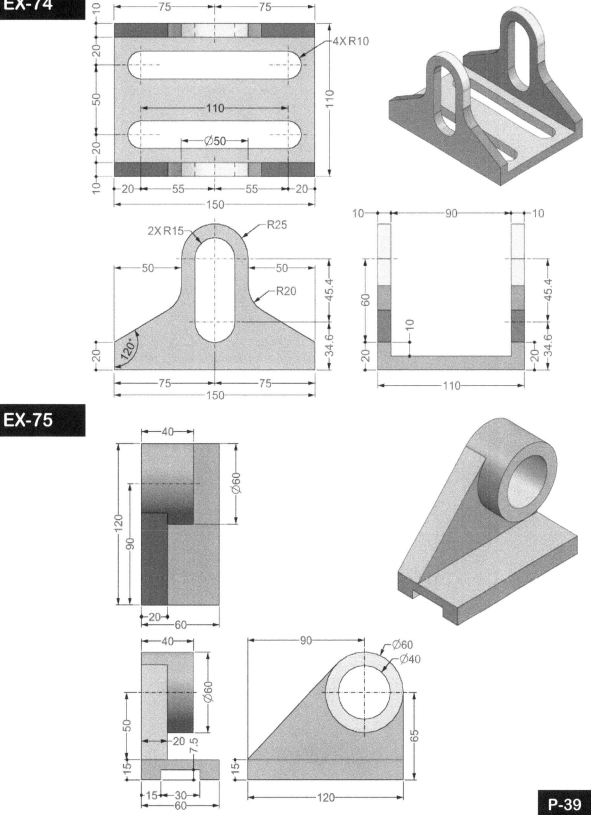

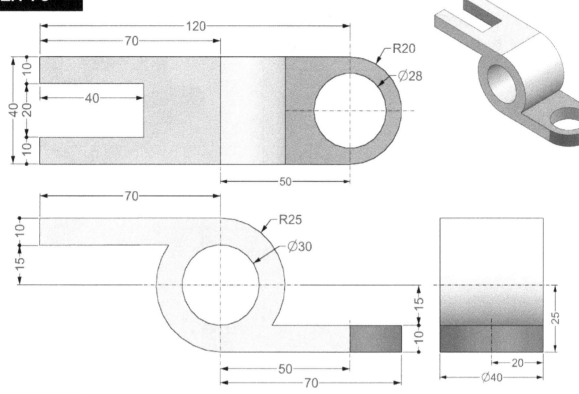

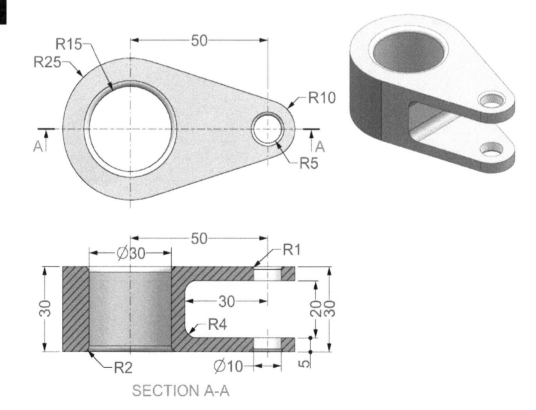

SECTION A-A

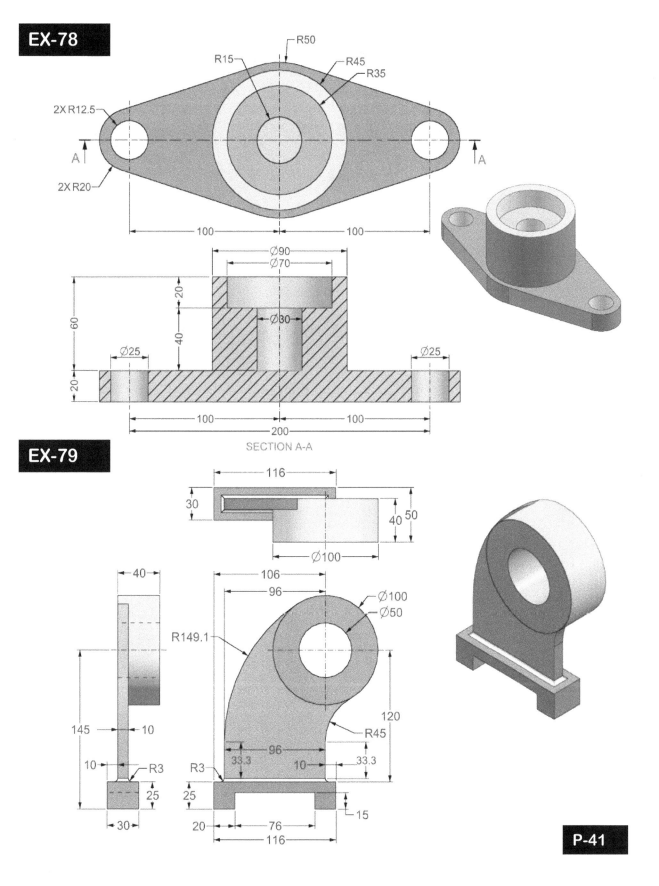

EX-78

R50
R15
R45
R35
2X R12.5
2X R20
A
A
100
100

∅90
∅70
20
60
40
∅30
∅25
∅25
20
100
100
200
SECTION A-A

EX-79

116
30
40
50
∅100

40
106
96
∅100
∅50
R149.1
145
10
10
R3
25
120
R45
96
33.3
10
33.3
R3
25
30
20
76
116
15

P-41

EX-80

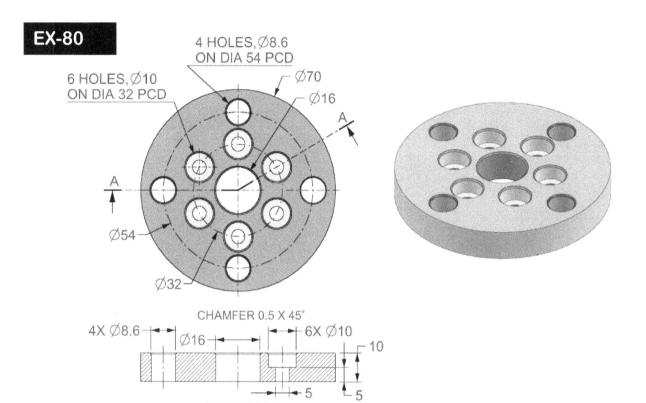

6 HOLES, Ø10
ON DIA 32 PCD

4 HOLES, Ø8.6
ON DIA 54 PCD

Ø70

Ø16

A

A

Ø54

Ø32

CHAMFER 0.5 X 45°

4X Ø8.6   Ø16   6X Ø10   10

5   5

SECTION A-A
(SCALE 1:1)

EX-81

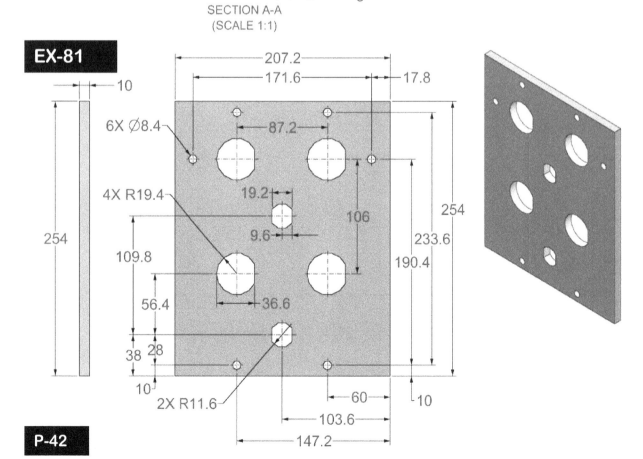

207.2

171.6   17.8

6X Ø8.4

87.2

4X R19.4

19.2

9.6

254

106

233.6

190.4

10

254

109.8

36.6

56.4

38   28

10

2X R11.6

60

10

103.6

147.2

P-42

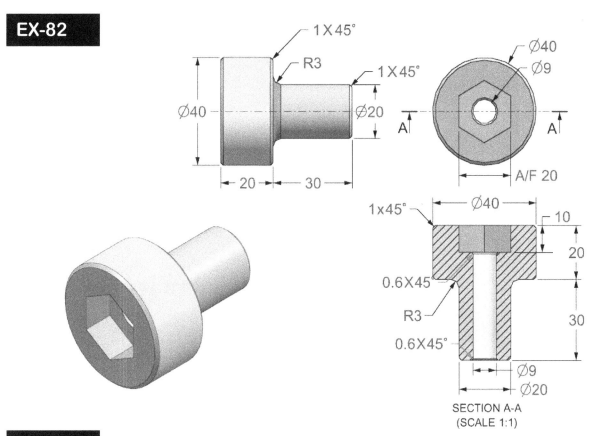

1 X 45°
R3
1 X 45°
⌀40
Ø20
20
30

⌀40
Ø9
A
A
A/F 20

1x45°
⌀40
10
20
0.6X45
R3
0.6X45°
Ø9
Ø20
30

SECTION A-A
(SCALE 1:1)

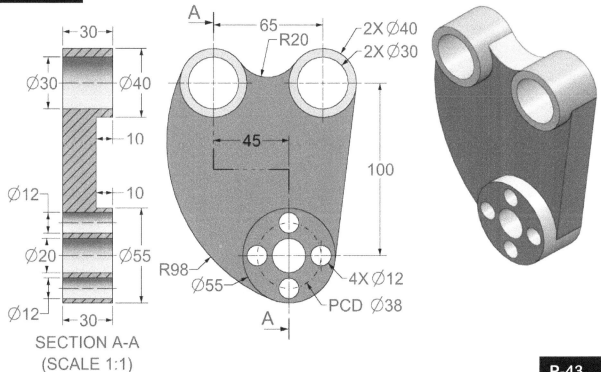

30
Ø30
Ø40
10
10
Ø12
Ø20
Ø55
Ø12
30

SECTION A-A
(SCALE 1:1)

A
65
R20
2X Ø40
2X Ø30
45
100
R98
Ø55
4X Ø12
PCD Ø38
A

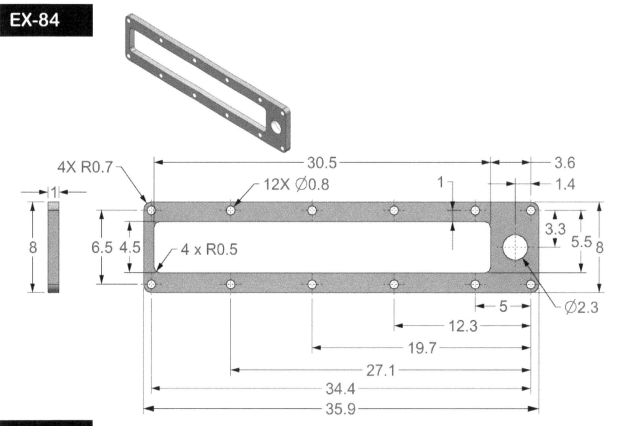

4X R0.7
12X Ø0.8
30.5
3.6
1.4
1
1
4 x R0.5
6.5 4.5
8
8
3.3
5.5
8
5
12.3
Ø2.3
19.7
27.1
34.4
35.9

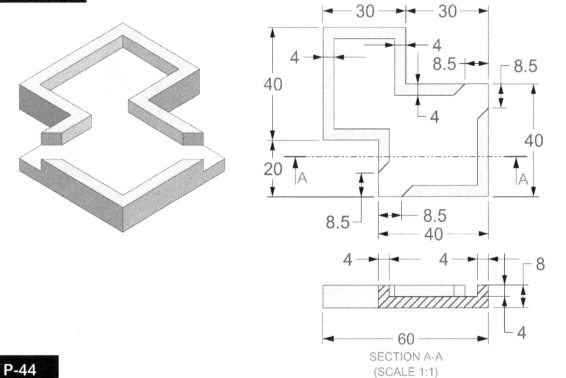

30
30
4
4
8.5
8.5
40
40
20
A
A
8.5
8.5
40
4
4
8
60
4
SECTION A-A
(SCALE 1:1)

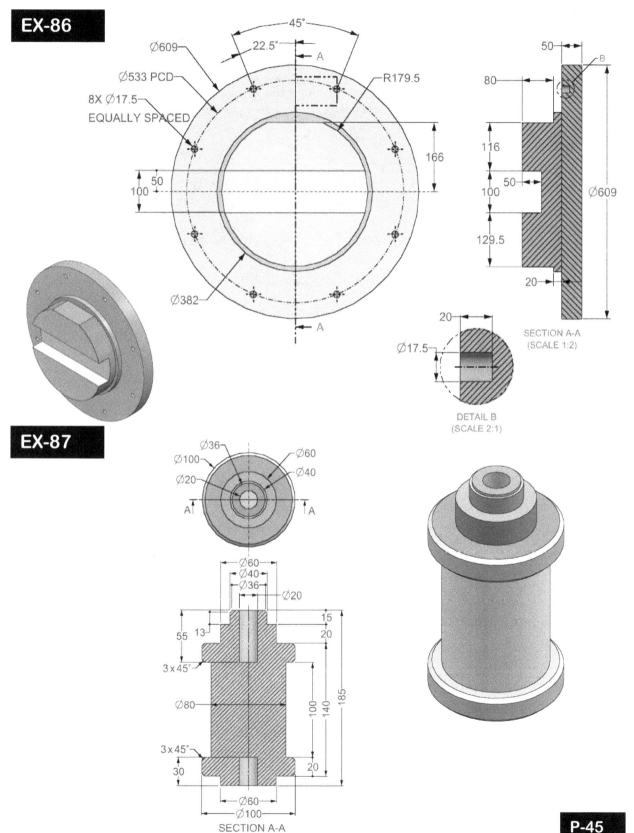

EX-86

∅609
∅533 PCD
8X ∅17.5
EQUALLY SPACED
45°
22.5°
A
R179.5
166
50
100
∅382
A

50
80
B
116
50
100
129.5
20
∅609

SECTION A-A
(SCALE 1:2)

20
∅17.5

DETAIL B
(SCALE 2:1)

EX-87

∅36
∅100
∅20
∅60
∅40
A   A

∅60
∅40
∅36
∅20
15
20
55
13
3 x 45°
∅80
100
140
185
3 x 45°
30
20
∅60
∅100
SECTION A-A

P-45

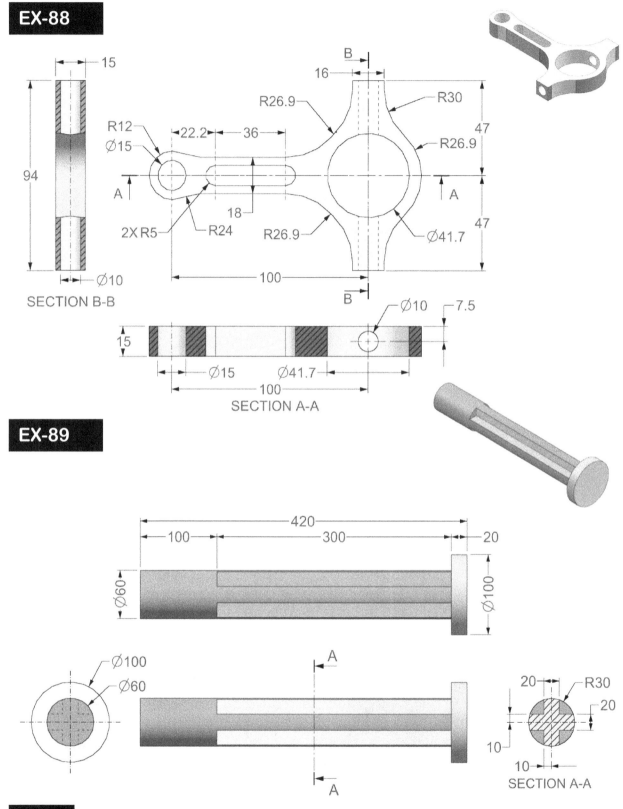

EX-88

R12
Ø15
22.2
36
R26.9
16
R30
B
R30
47
R26.9
2X R5
R24
18
R26.9
Ø41.7
47
100

15
94
Ø10
SECTION B-B

Ø10
7.5
15
Ø15
Ø41.7
100
SECTION A-A

EX-89

420
100
300
20
Ø60
Ø100

Ø100
Ø60
A
A

20
R30
20
10
10
SECTION A-A

P-46

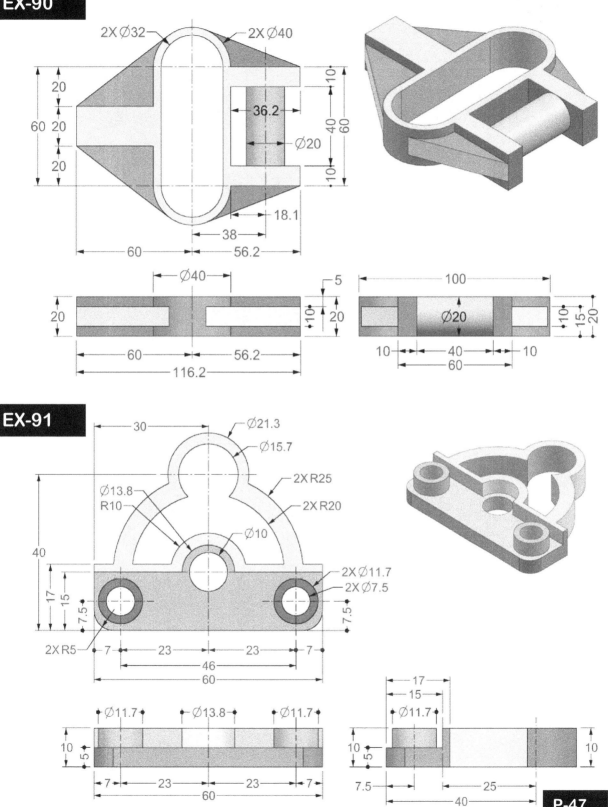

EX-90

2X Ø32   2X Ø40

20
60 20
20

36.2
Ø20

10
40
60
10

18.1
38
60   56.2

Ø40
20
60   56.2
116.2

5
10   20

100
Ø20
10   40   10
60
10
15
20

EX-91

30
Ø21.3
Ø15.7
2X R25
Ø13.8
R10
2X R20
Ø10
40
17
15
7.5
2X Ø11.7
2X Ø7.5
7.5
2X R5   7   23   23   7
46
60

Ø11.7   Ø13.8   Ø11.7
10
5
7   23   23   7
60

17
15
Ø11.7
10
5
7.5   25
40
10

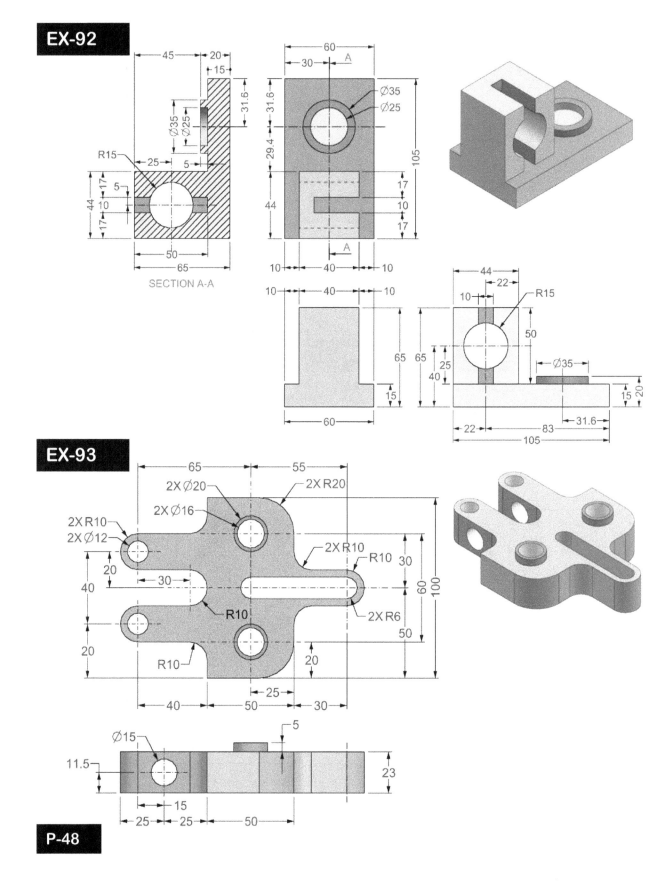

EX-92

45 | 20
15
Ø35
Ø25
31.6
R15
25 | 5
44
17
5
10
17
50
65
SECTION A-A

60
30 | A
31.6
Ø35
Ø25
29.4
44
17
10
17
A
10 | 40 | 10
105

10 | 40 | 10
65
15
60

44
22
10
R15
50
65
25
40
Ø35
15
20
22
83
31.6
105

EX-93

65 | 55
2X Ø20
2X R20
2X Ø16
2X R10
2X Ø12
2X R10
R10
30
20
60
100
30
2X R10
40
R10
2X R6
20
50
R10
20
25
40 | 50 | 30

Ø15
5
11.5
23
15
25 | 25 | 50

P-48

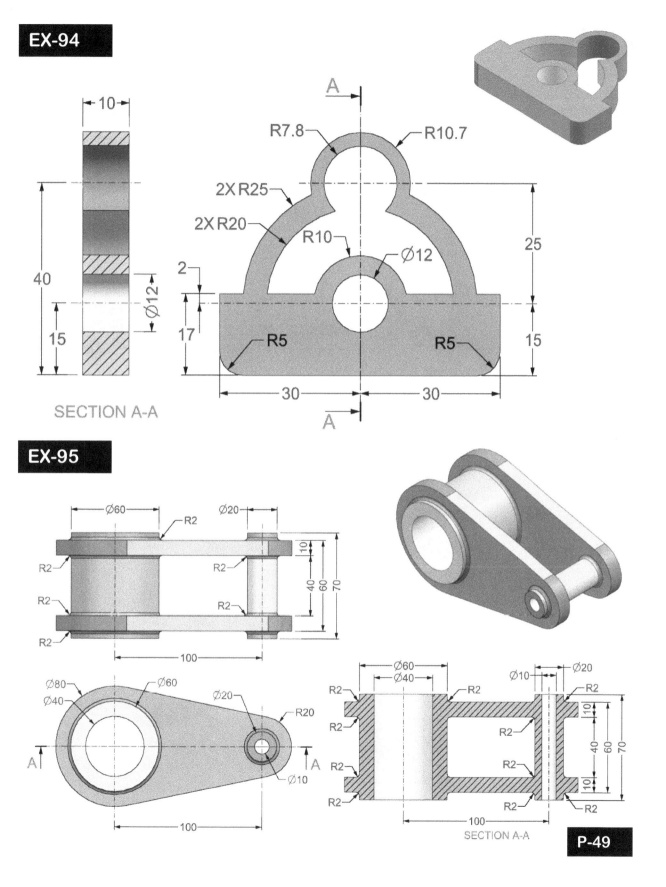

EX-94

10

40

15

Ø12

SECTION A-A

A

R7.8   R10.7

2X R25

2X R20

R10   Ø12

2

17

R5   R5

25

15

30   30

A

EX-95

Ø60   R2   Ø20

R2

R2

R2   R2

R2   R2

10
40
60
70

100

Ø80   Ø60   Ø20
Ø40   R20

A   A

Ø10

100

Ø60
Ø40
R2   R2

R2

Ø10   Ø20
R2

10
40
60
70

R2   R2

R2

R2   R2   R2

100

SECTION A-A

P-49

EX-96

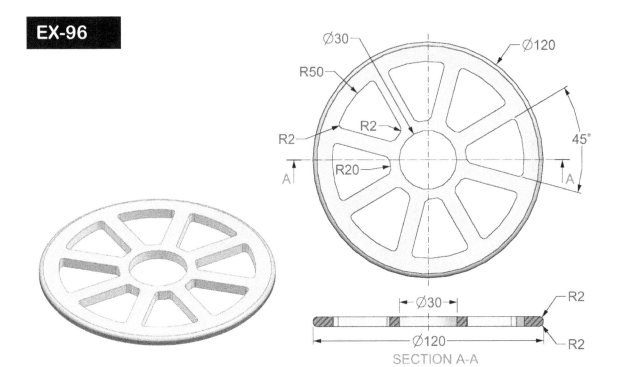

Ø30
Ø120
R50
R2
R2
R2
R20
45°
A
A

Ø30
Ø120
R2
R2
SECTION A-A

EX-97

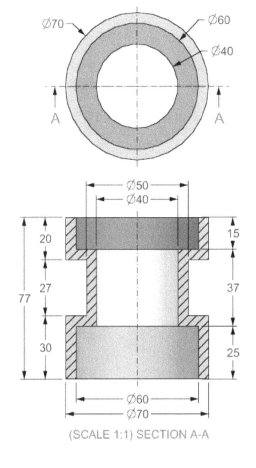

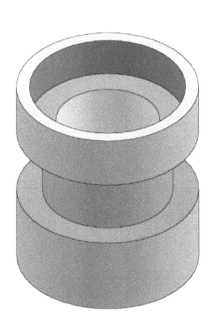

Ø70
Ø60
Ø40
A
A

Ø50
Ø40
20
15
27
37
77
30
25
Ø60
Ø70

(SCALE 1:1) SECTION A-A

P-50

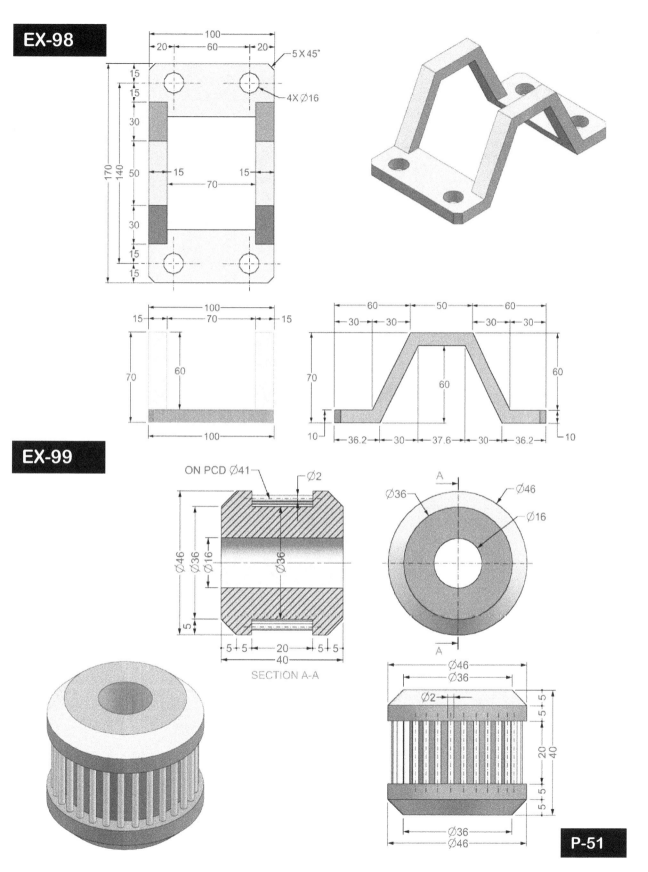

EX-98

EX-99

ON PCD Ø41

SECTION A-A

P-51

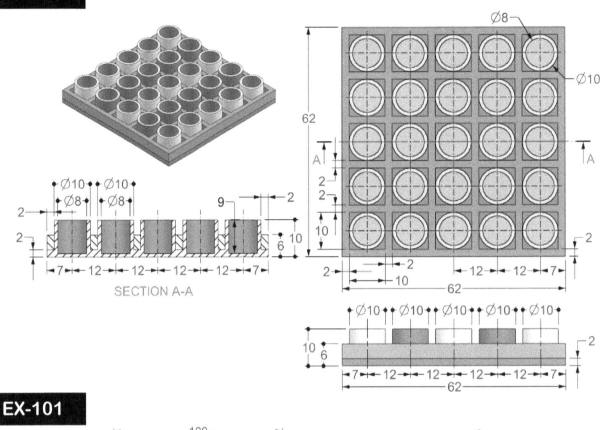

SECTION A-A

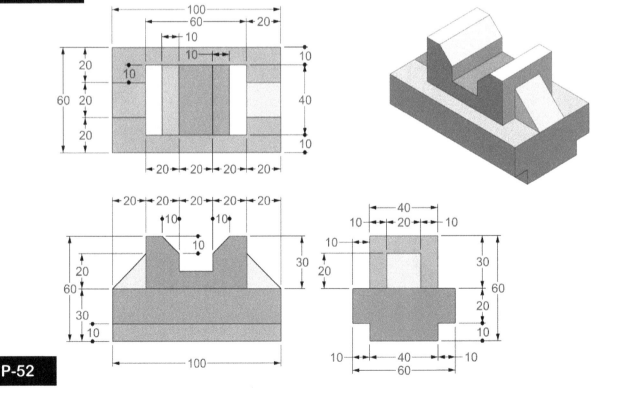

EX-102

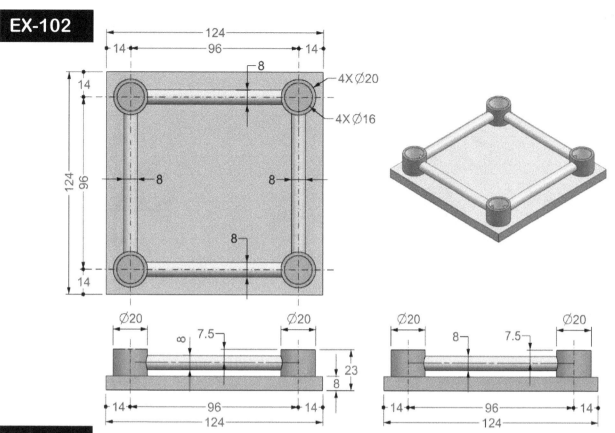

EX-103

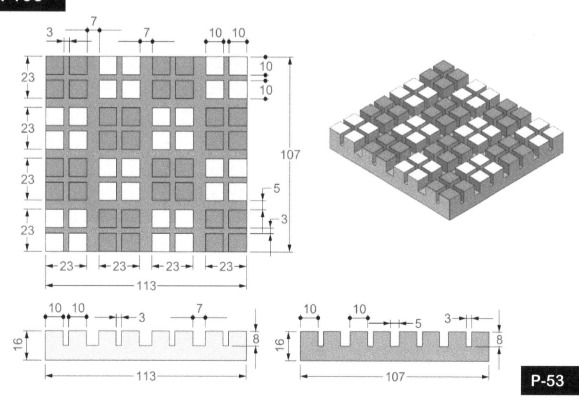

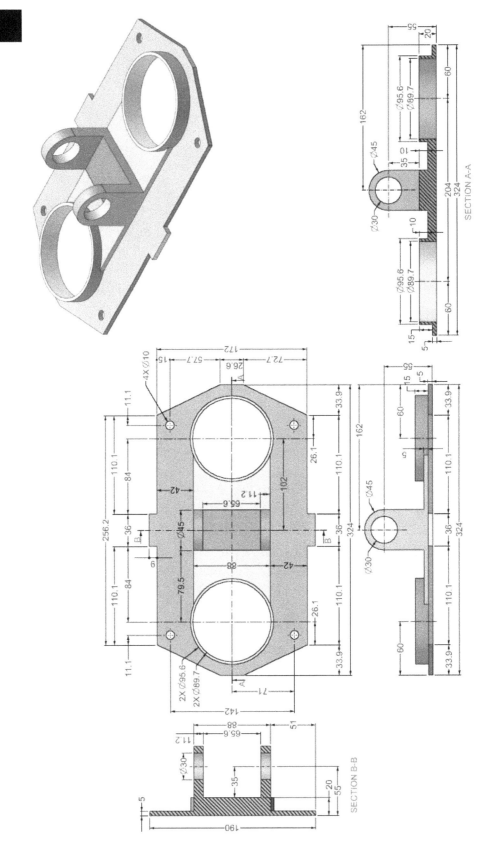

SECTION A-A

SECTION B-B

EX-105

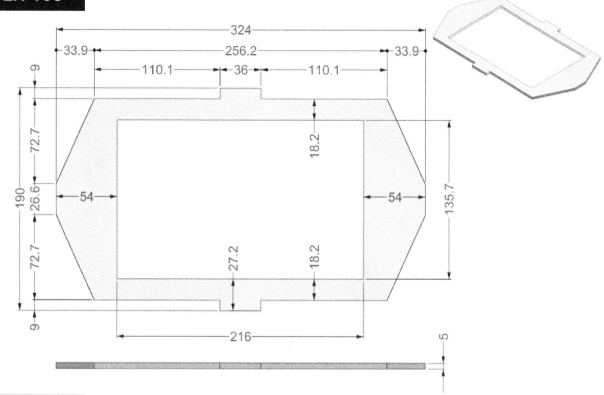

EX-106

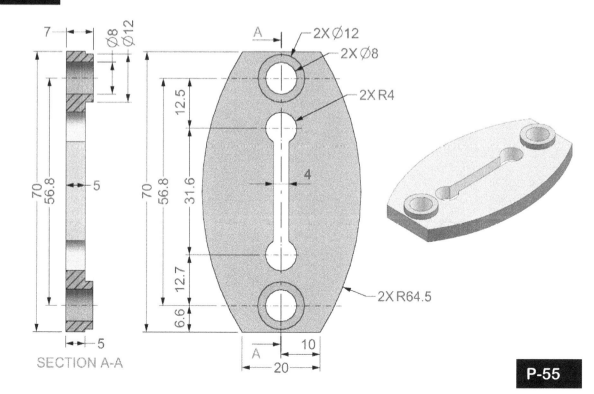

SECTION A-A

EX-107

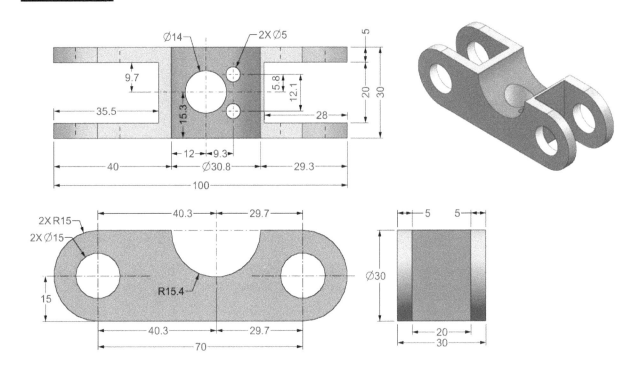

EX-108

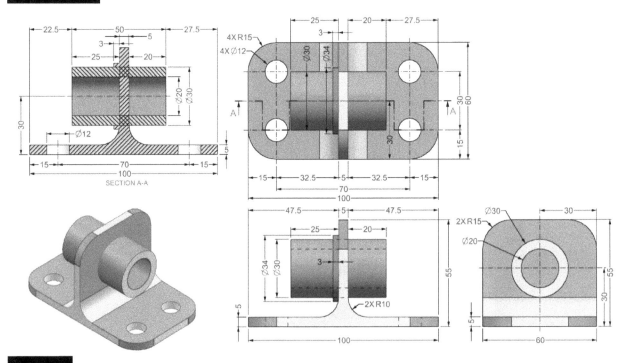

SECTION A-A

P-56

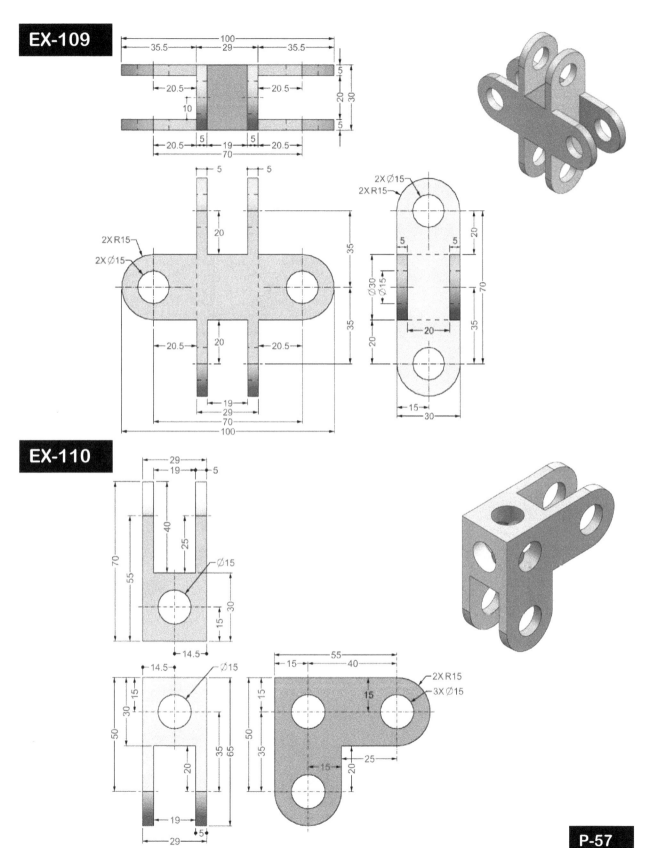

EX-109

EX-110

EX-111

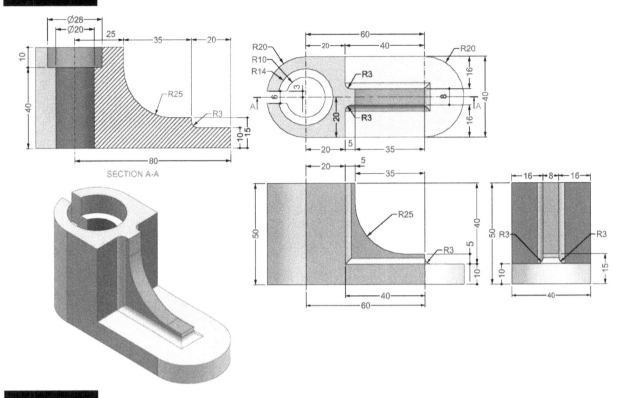

SECTION A-A

EX-112

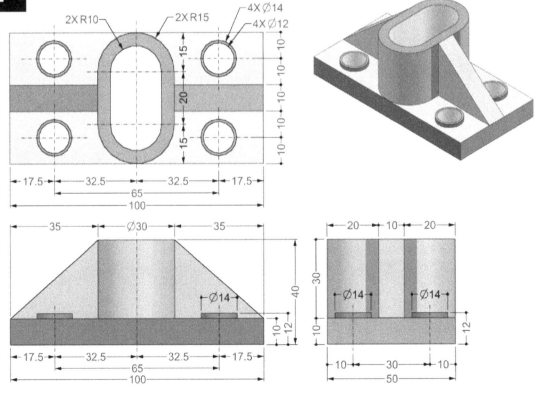

P-58

EX-113

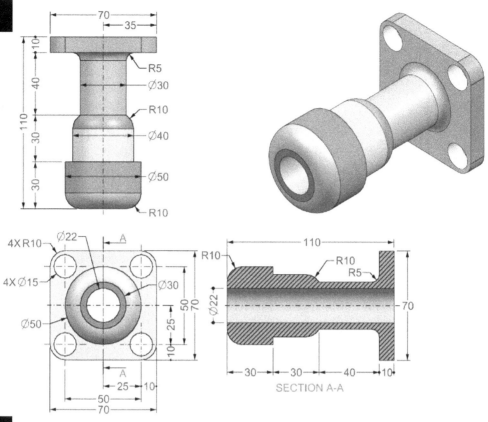

SECTION A-A

EX-114

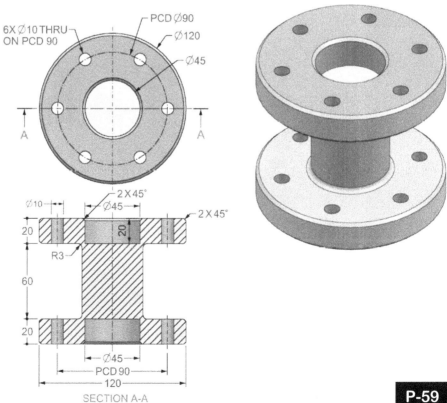

SECTION A-A

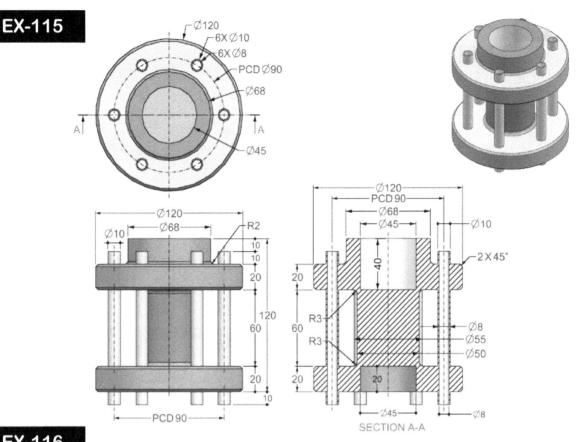

SECTION A-A

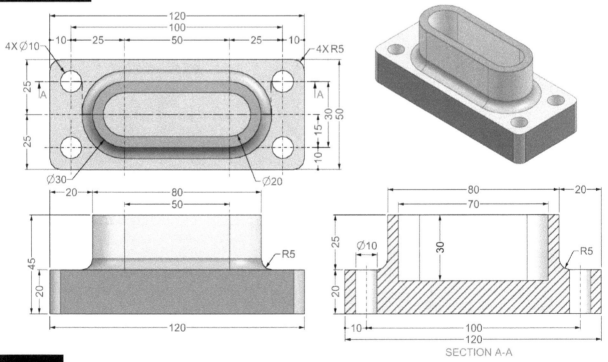

SECTION A-A

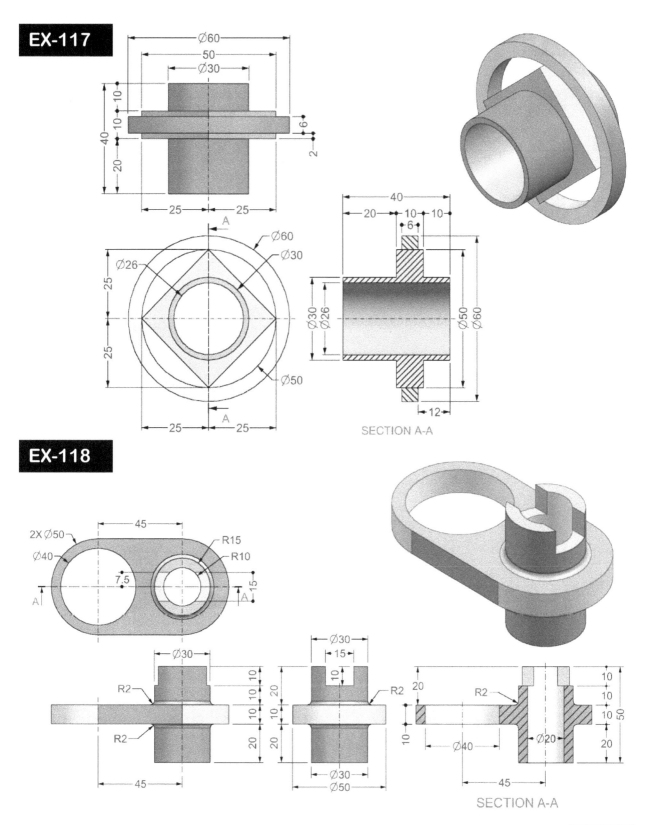

EX-117

⌀60
50
⌀30
10
10
40
20
6
2
25 25

A

⌀60
⌀30
⌀26
25
25
⌀50
25 25
A

40
20 10 10
6
⌀30
⌀26
⌀50
⌀60
12

SECTION A-A

EX-118

2X ⌀50
⌀40
45
R15
R10
7.5
15
A
A

⌀30
R2
R2
10 10
10
20
10
10
20
45

⌀30
15
10
R2
20
10
20
⌀30
⌀50

20
R2
⌀40
⌀20
45
10
10
10
20
50
10

SECTION A-A

P-61

EX-119

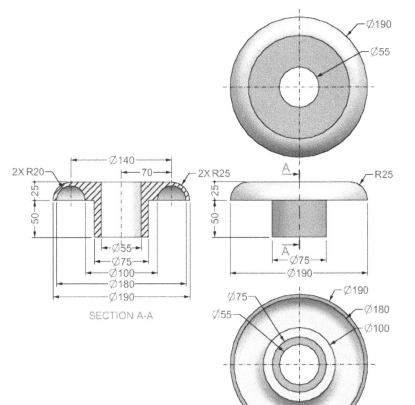

Ø140
70
2X R20
2X R25
25
50
Ø55
Ø75
Ø100
Ø180
Ø190

SECTION A-A

Ø190
Ø55

A
R25
25
50
Ø75
Ø190

Ø75
Ø190
Ø55
Ø180
Ø100

EX-120

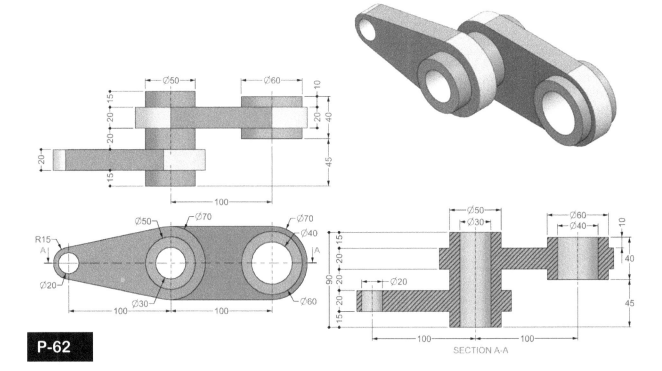

Ø50
Ø60
10
15
20
20
20
40
20
20
15
45
100

R15
A
Ø50
Ø70
Ø70
Ø40
A
Ø20
Ø30
Ø60
100
100

Ø50
Ø30
Ø60
Ø40
10
15
20
20
40
90
20
Ø20
15
20
45
100
100

SECTION A-A

P-62

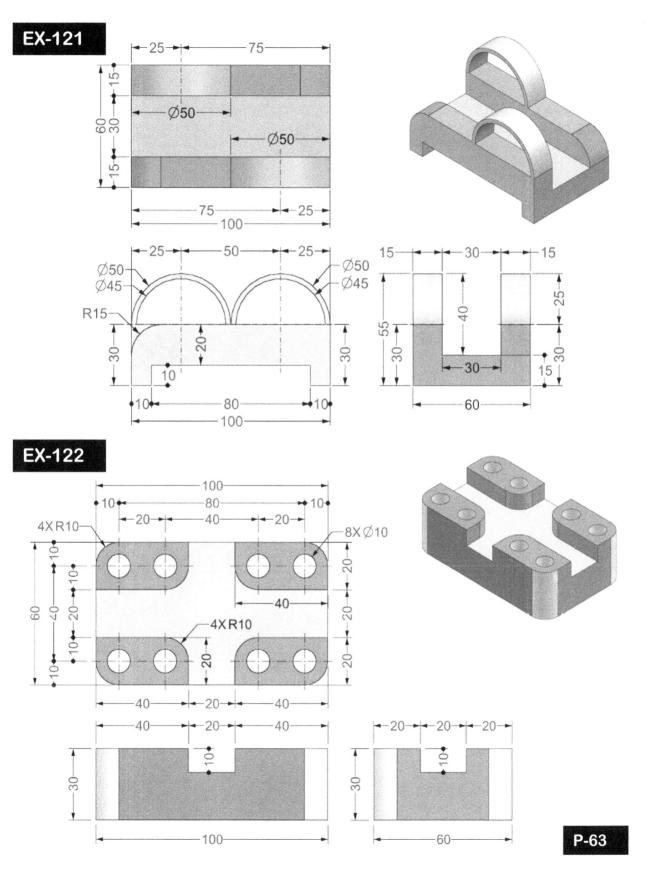

EX-121

EX-122

P-63

EX-123

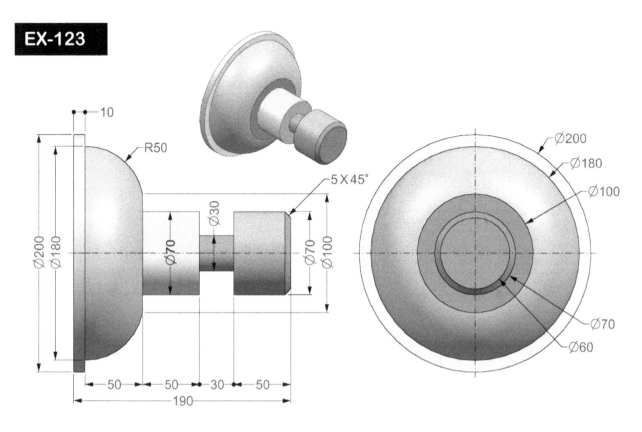

10
R50
5 X 45°
Ø30
Ø70
Ø70
Ø100
Ø200
Ø180
50 50 30 50
190

Ø200
Ø180
Ø100
Ø70
Ø60

EX-124

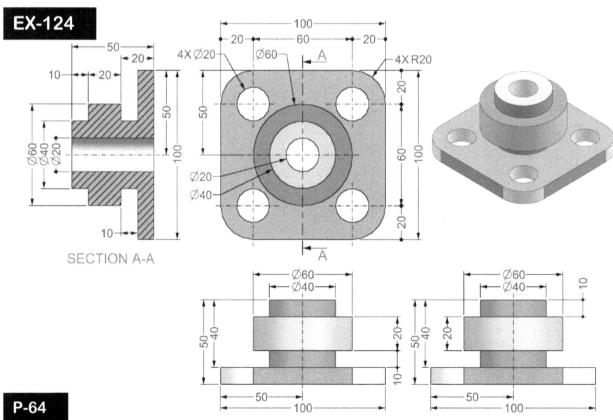

50
20
10 20
Ø60
Ø40
Ø20
50
100
10

SECTION A-A

100
20 60 20
4X Ø20
Ø60
A
4X R20
50
20
60
100
Ø20
Ø40
20
A

Ø60
Ø40
50
40
20
50
100
10

Ø60
Ø40
50
40
20
50
100
10

P-64

EX-125

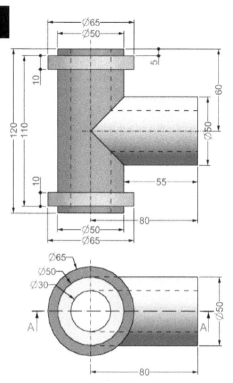

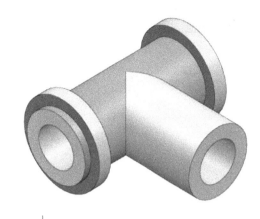

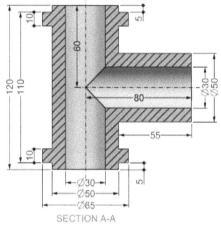

SECTION A-A

EX-126

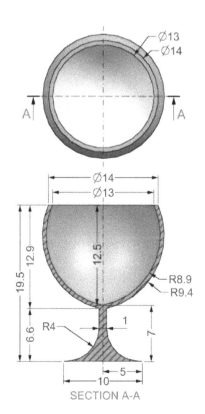

SECTION A-A

P-65

EX-127

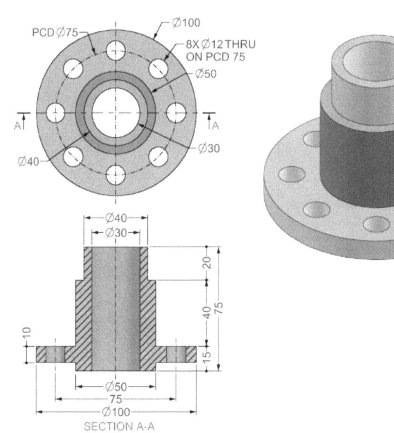

PCD Ø75
Ø100
8X Ø12 THRU
ON PCD 75
Ø50
A
A
Ø40
Ø30

Ø40
Ø30
20
75
40
10
15
Ø50
75
Ø100
SECTION A-A

EX-128

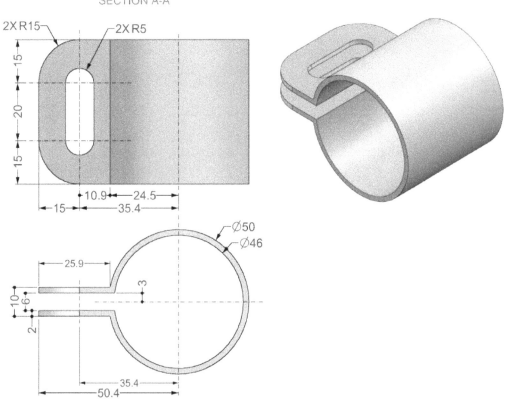

2X R15
2X R5
15
20
15
10.9
24.5
15
35.4

Ø50
Ø46
25.9
10
6
3
2
35.4
50.4

EX-129

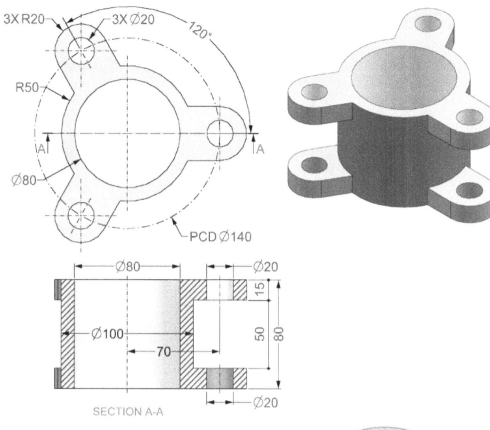

3X R20 3X Ø20 120°

R50

A ← → A

Ø80

PCD Ø140

Ø80 Ø20

15

Ø100

70

50 80

Ø20

SECTION A-A

EX-130

PCD Ø55 Ø70

A ← → A

8X Ø8
ON PCD 55

Ø30 Ø40

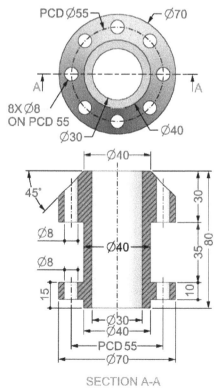

Ø40

45°

30

Ø8

Ø40

80

Ø8

35

15

10

Ø30
Ø40
PCD 55
Ø70

SECTION A-A

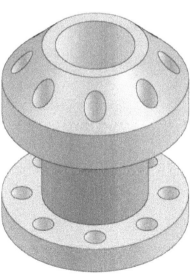

EX-131

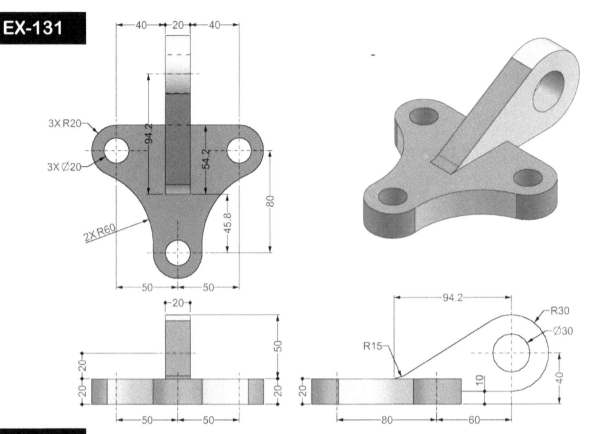

3X R20
3X Ø20
2X R60

40 20 40
94.2
54.2
80
45.8
50 50

20
50
20 20 20
50 50

94.2
R30
Ø30
R15
20 10 40
80 60

EX-132

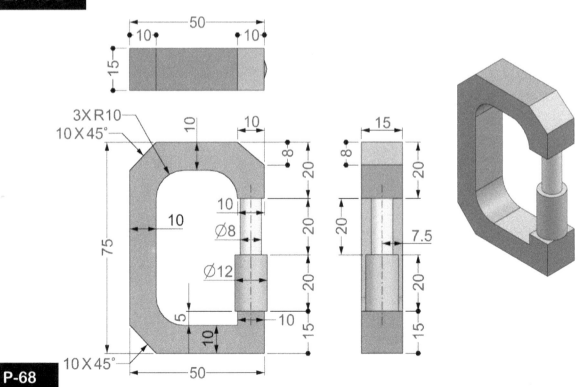

50
10 10
15

3X R10
10 X 45°
10
10
8
20
10
Ø8
20
10
Ø12
20
75
5
10
10
50
10 X 45°
15

15
8
20
20
20
7.5
20
15

P-68

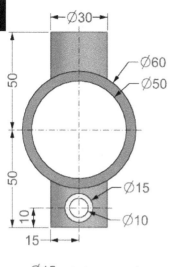

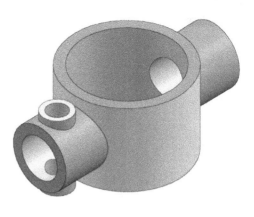

Ø30
Ø60
Ø50
50
50
Ø15
Ø10
10
15

Ø30
Ø15
Ø20
Ø15
Ø60
30
20
36
40
18
30
Ø60
36
18
Ø30
40
Ø30
10
40
50
20

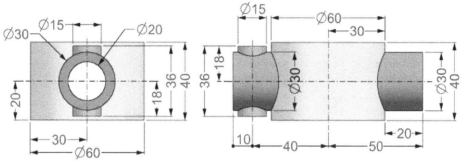

Ø40
Ø120
Ø60
A
A

80
70
50
2 X 45°
R30
Ø120
Ø60
Ø93.2
Ø60
Ø120
5
10
10
5

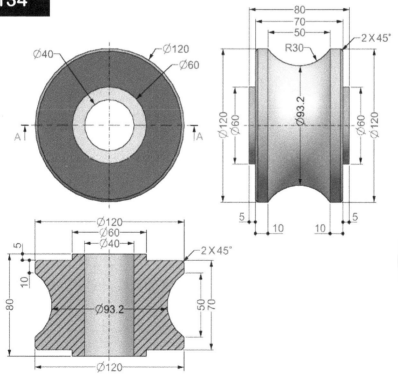

Ø120
Ø60
Ø40
2 X 45°
5
10
80
Ø93.2
50
70
Ø120

SECTION A-A

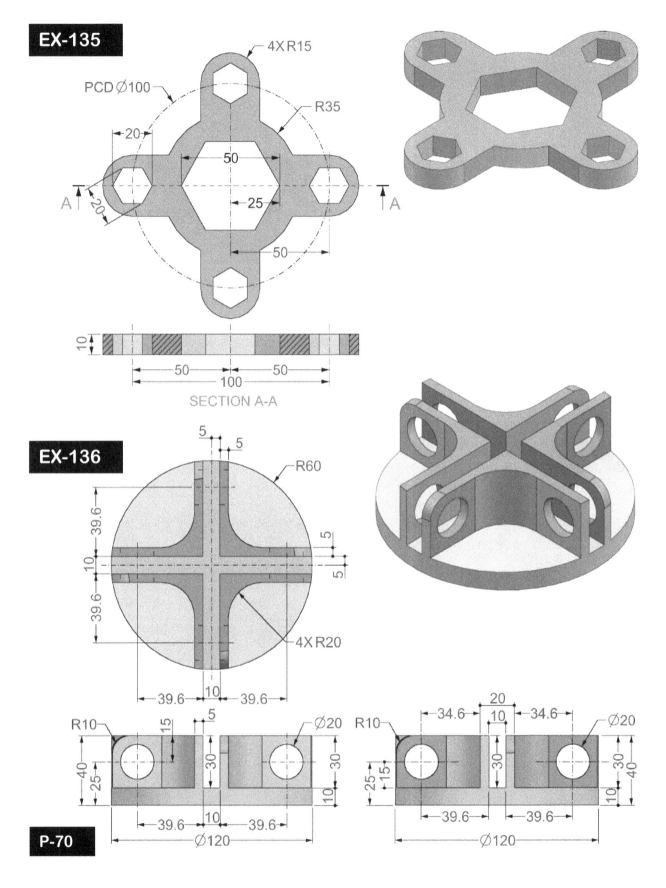

EX-135

4X R15

PCD ⌀100

R35

20

50

25

50

20

A — A

10

50 — 50
100

SECTION A-A

EX-136

5

5

R60

39.6

10

39.6

5

5

4X R20

39.6 — 10 — 39.6

R10

15

5

⌀20

40

30

25

30

10

39.6 — 10 — 39.6

⌀120

20

34.6 — 10 — 34.6

R10

⌀20

25

15

30

30

40

10

39.6 — 39.6

⌀120

P-70

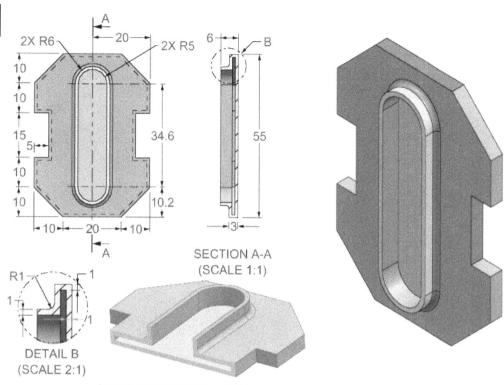

EX-137

2X R6
2X R5
20
6
B
10
10
15
5
34.6
55
10
10
10.2
10
20
10
3
A

SECTION A-A
(SCALE 1:1)

R1
1
1
1

DETAIL B
(SCALE 2:1)

SHELL THICKNESS = 1MM
ALL INSIDE WALL THICKNESS

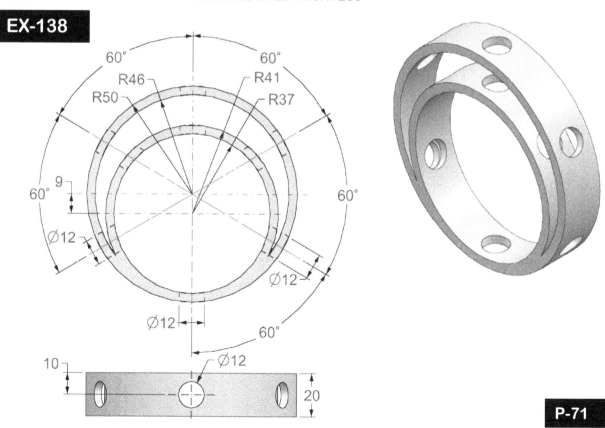

EX-138

60°   60°
R46   R41
R50   R37
60°   60°
9
Ø12
Ø12
60°
Ø12
Ø12
10
Ø12
20

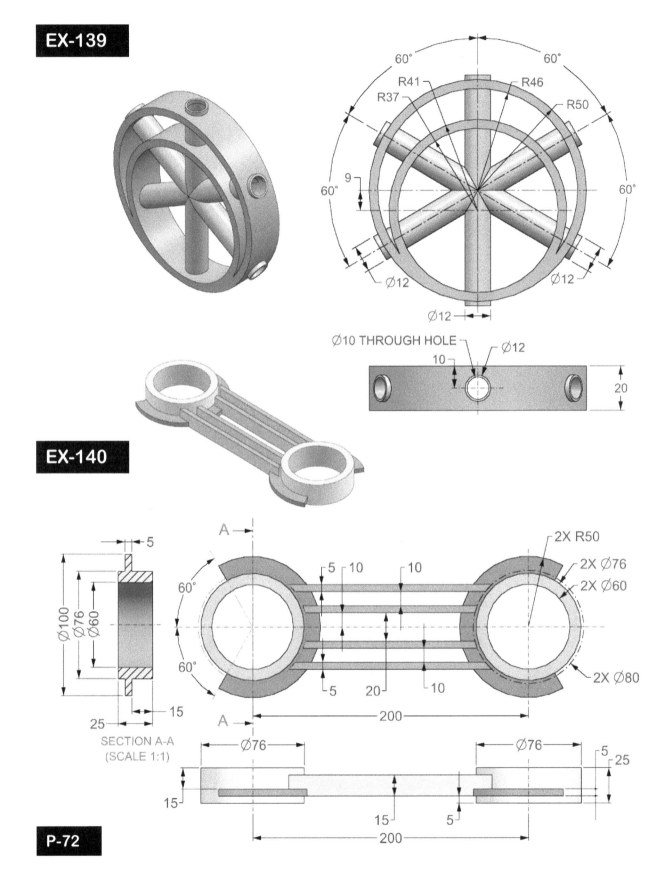

EX-139

60° 60°
R41 R46
R37 R50
60° 9 60°
60° 60°
⌀12 ⌀12
⌀12

⌀10 THROUGH HOLE ⌀12
10
20

EX-140

A

2X R50
5 10 10
2X ⌀76
60° 2X ⌀60

⌀100 ⌀76 ⌀60

60°
5 20 10 2X ⌀80
15
25 A

5

SECTION A-A
(SCALE 1:1)

200

⌀76 ⌀76
5 25
15 15 5
15
200

P-72

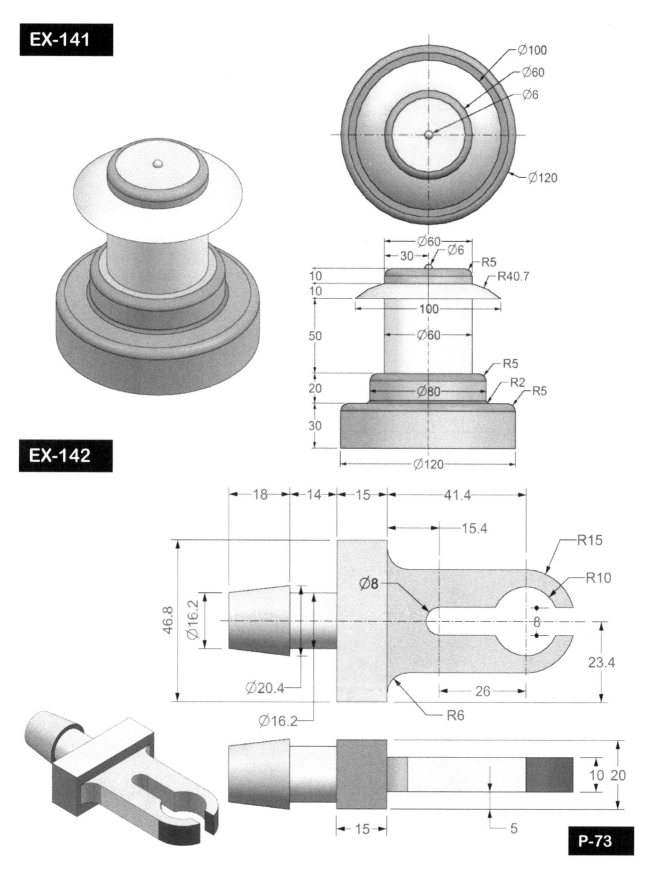

EX-141

Ø100
Ø60
Ø6
Ø120

Ø60
30
Ø6
R5
R40.7
10
10
100
Ø60
50
R5
20
Ø80
R2 R5
30
Ø120

EX-142

18
14
15
41.4
15.4
R15
R10
Ø8
46.8
Ø16.2
8
Ø20.4
23.4
Ø16.2
R6
26

10 20
15
5

P-73

EX-143

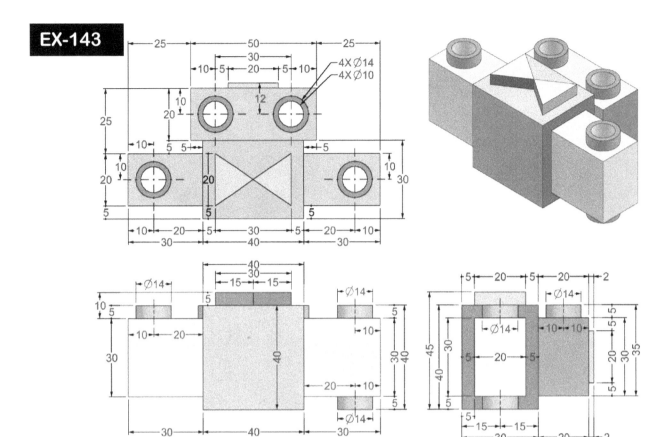

EX-144

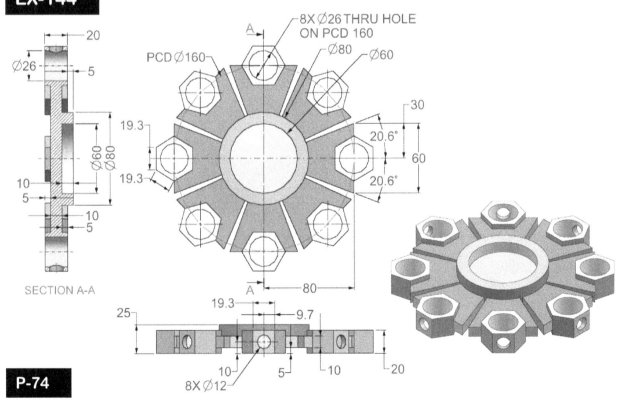

SECTION A-A

8X Ø26 THRU HOLE ON PCD 160

PCD Ø160

Ø80

Ø60

8X Ø12

P-74

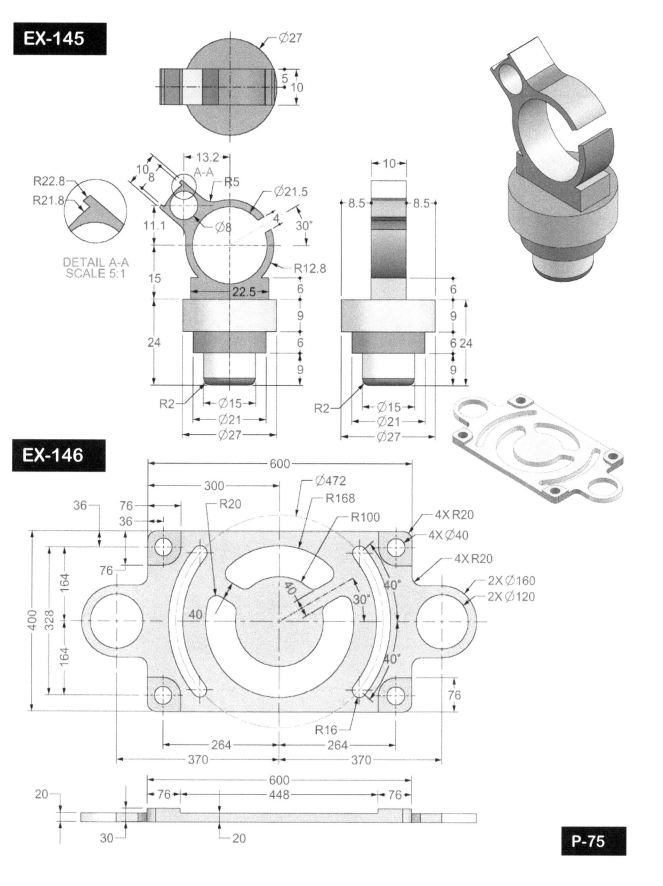

EX-145

⌀27
5
10

R22.8
R21.8

R5
10
8
13.2
A-A
⌀21.5
11.1
⌀8
4
30°
DETAIL A-A
SCALE 5:1
R12.8
15
22.5
6
9
6
24
9
R2
⌀15
⌀21
⌀27

10
8.5
8.5
6
9
6 24
9
R2
⌀15
⌀21
⌀27

EX-146

600
300
⌀472
R168
R20
R100
4X R20
36
76
36
4X ⌀40
76
4X R20
164
2X ⌀160
2X ⌀120
400
328
40
40
30°
40°
164
40
40°
76
R16
264
264
370
370

600
76
448
76
20
30
20

P-75

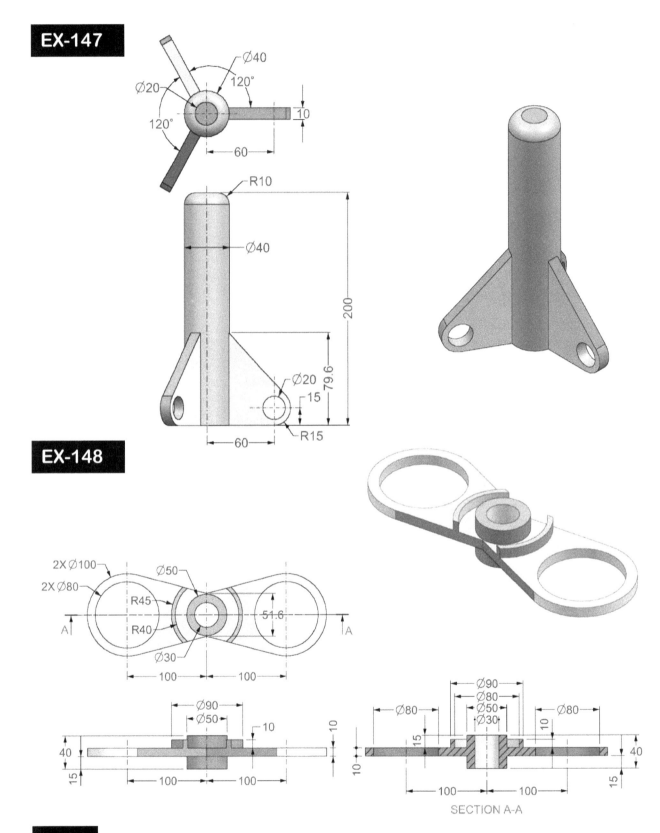

EX-147

Ø40
Ø20
120°
120°
10
60

R10
Ø40
200
79.6
Ø20
15
60
R15

EX-148

2X Ø100
2X Ø80
Ø50
R45
R40
Ø30
51.6
A
A
100
100

Ø90
Ø50
10
10
40
15
100
100

Ø90
Ø80
Ø50
Ø30
Ø80
Ø80
15
10
10
40
15
100
100

SECTION A-A

P-76

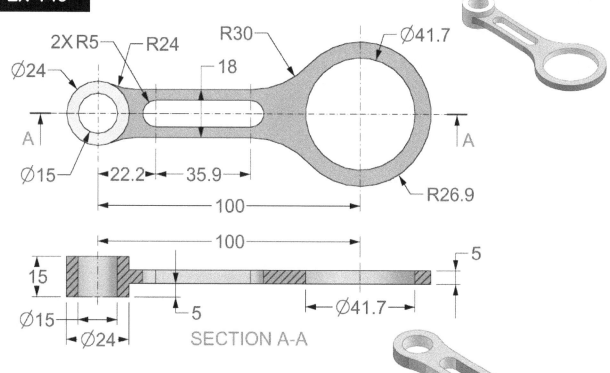

2X R5 — R24   R30   Ø41.7

Ø24

18

100

SECTION A-A

15

Ø15

Ø24

5

Ø41.7

22.2   35.9

100

R26.9

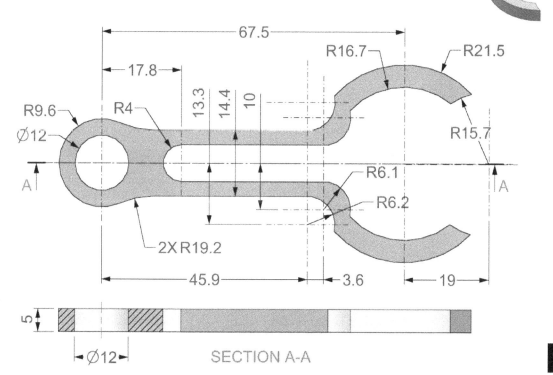

67.5

17.8

R16.7   R21.5

13.3   14.4   10

R9.6

Ø12

R4

R15.7

R6.1

R6.2

2X R19.2

45.9   3.6   19

5

Ø12

SECTION A-A

Ø8

6.5

10

28

R1.5

R1.5

11

B-B

27

Ø10

SECTION A-A

Ø20

A

R3

35

15°

20

5

A

Ø13.3

Ø16

R8

R10

R6.7

R4

R5

DETAIL B-B
SCALE 5:1

1

45°

Ø20
Ø36

Ø58

Ø52

Ø16

Ø36

Ø20

R8

8

20

2

135°

Ø16

13.5

R11.2

15.8

76

10.7

21.6

13

R6

Ø16

R3

10

A

58

3

R3

R2

Ø52

76

R6

A

40

SECTION A-A

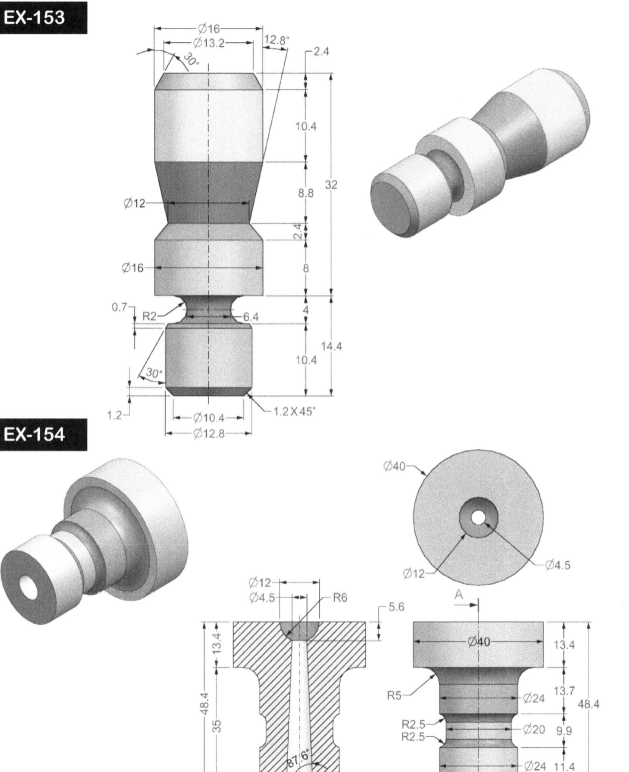

EX-153

EX-154

SECTION A-A

P-79

EX-155

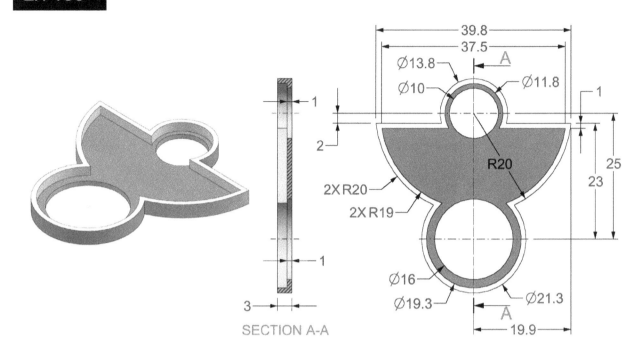

Ø13.8
Ø10
Ø11.8
39.8
37.5
A
1
2
R20
25
23
2X R20
2X R19
Ø16
Ø19.3
Ø21.3
19.9
1
3
SECTION A-A

EX-156

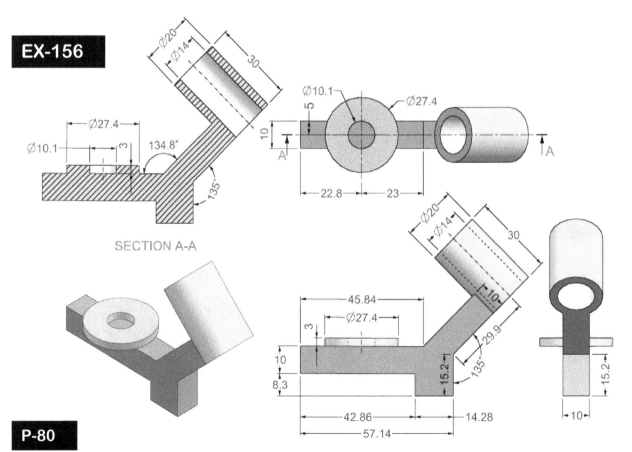

Ø20
Ø14
30
Ø27.4
Ø10.1
3
134.8°
135°
SECTION A-A

Ø10.1
Ø27.4
5
10
22.8
23

Ø20
Ø14
30
10
135°
29.9

45.84
Ø27.4
3
10
8.3
15.2
42.86
14.28
57.14

15.2
10

P-80

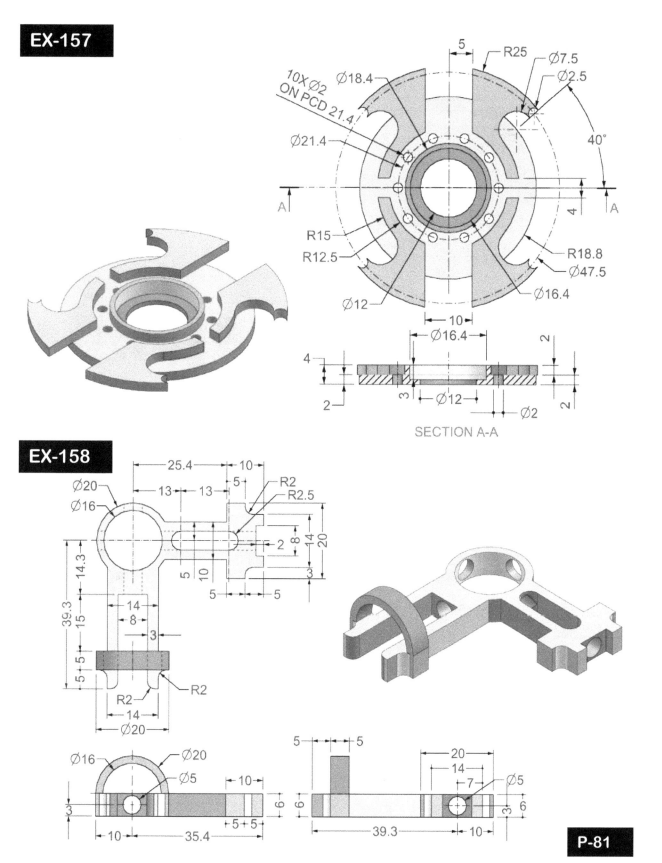

EX-157

10X Ø2
ON PCD 21.4

5

R25

Ø7.5

Ø2.5

Ø18.4

Ø21.4

40°

4

A

A

R15

R12.5

R18.8

Ø47.5

Ø12

Ø16.4

10

Ø16.4

2

4

3

Ø12

Ø2

2

2

SECTION A-A

EX-158

25.4

10

13

13

5

R2

R2.5

Ø20

Ø16

2

8

14

20

14.3

39.3

5

10

3

14

8

3

15

5

5

5

5

R2

R2

14

Ø20

Ø16

Ø20

Ø5

10

3

5+5

10

35.4

6

5

5

6

20

14

7

Ø5

6

39.3

10

3

6

P-81

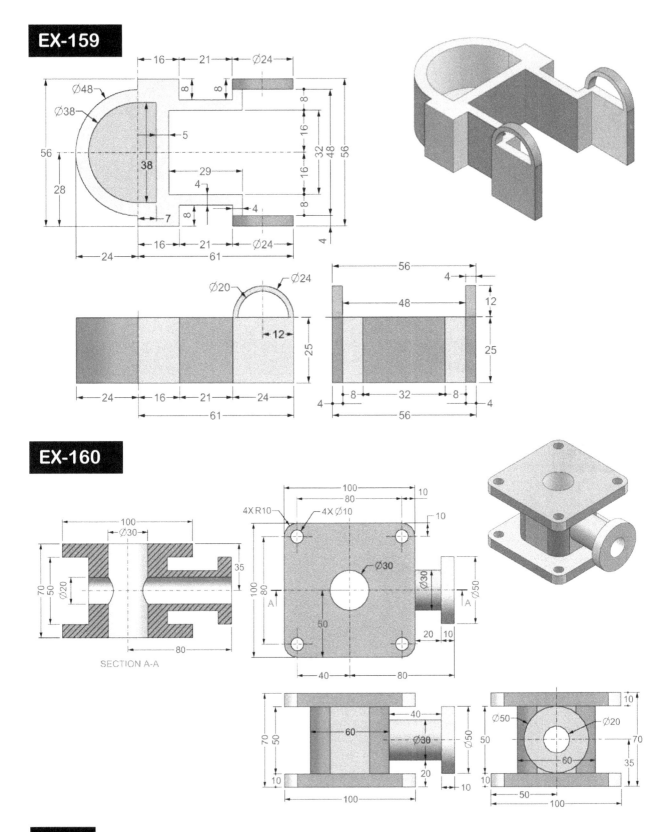

EX-159

EX-160

SECTION A-A

4X R10 4X Ø10

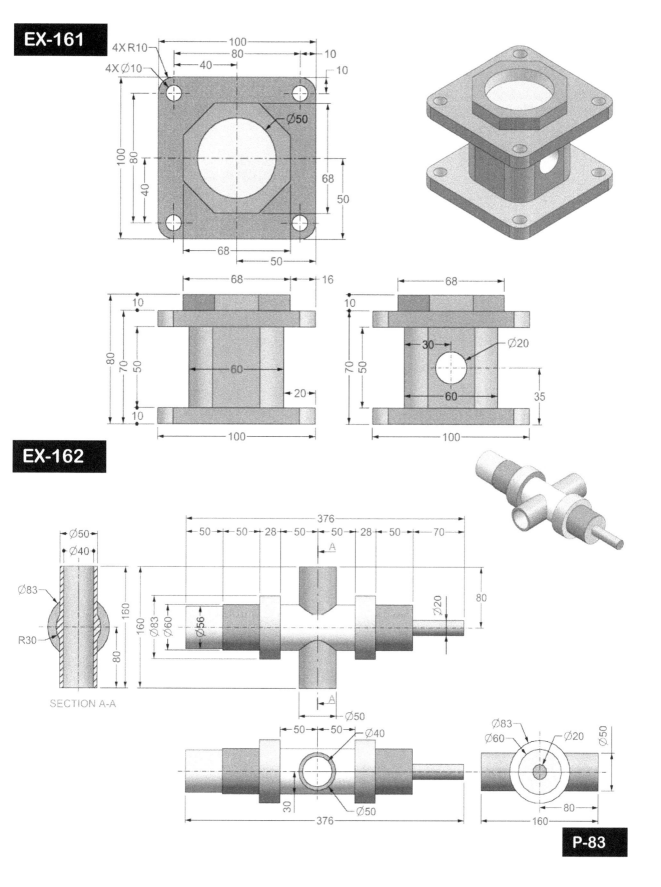

EX-161

4X R10
4X Ø10
100
80
40
10
10
Ø50
100
80
40
68
50
68
50

68
16
10
80
70
50
60
20
10
100

68
10
70
50
30
Ø20
60
35
100

EX-162

Ø50
Ø40
Ø83
R30
160
160
80
80
SECTION A-A

376
50 50 28 50 50 28 50 70
A
Ø83
Ø60
Ø56
Ø20
80
A
Ø50

50 50
Ø40
Ø50
30
Ø50
376

Ø83
Ø60
Ø20
Ø50
80
160

P-83

EX-163

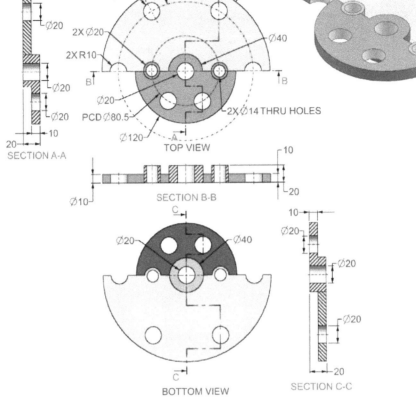

PCD Ø160
4X Ø20
2X Ø20
2X R10
Ø20
PCD Ø80.5
Ø120

R100
Ø40
2X Ø14 THRU HOLES

TOP VIEW

10
Ø20
Ø20
Ø20
20 · 10

SECTION A-A

10
20
Ø10

SECTION B-B

C
Ø20
Ø40

BOTTOM VIEW

10
Ø20
Ø20
Ø20
20

SECTION C-C

EX-164

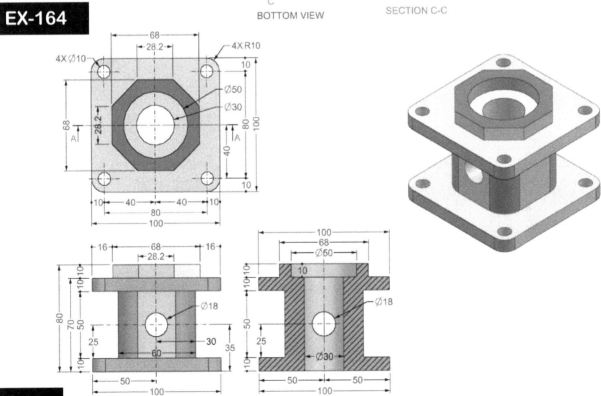

68
28.2
4X Ø10
4X R10
10
Ø50
Ø30
68
28.2
A
80
100
40
A
10
10 · 40 · 40 · 10
80
100

16 · 68 · 16
28.2
10 10
80
70
50
25
10
50
Ø18
30
60
35
50
100

100
68
Ø50
10 10
10
50
25
10
Ø18
Ø30
50 · 50
100

SECTION A-A

P-84

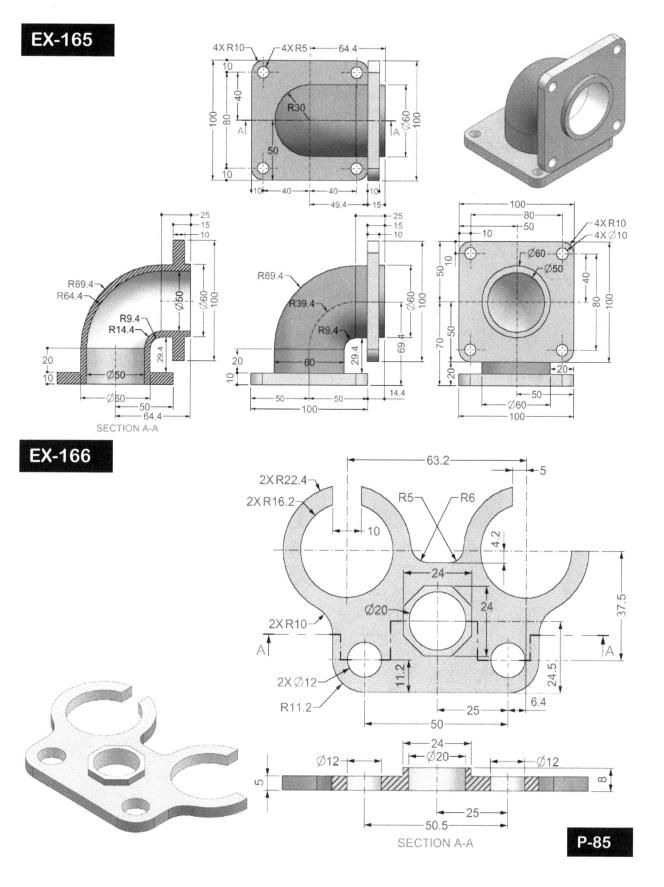

EX-165

SECTION A-A

EX-166

SECTION A-A

P-85

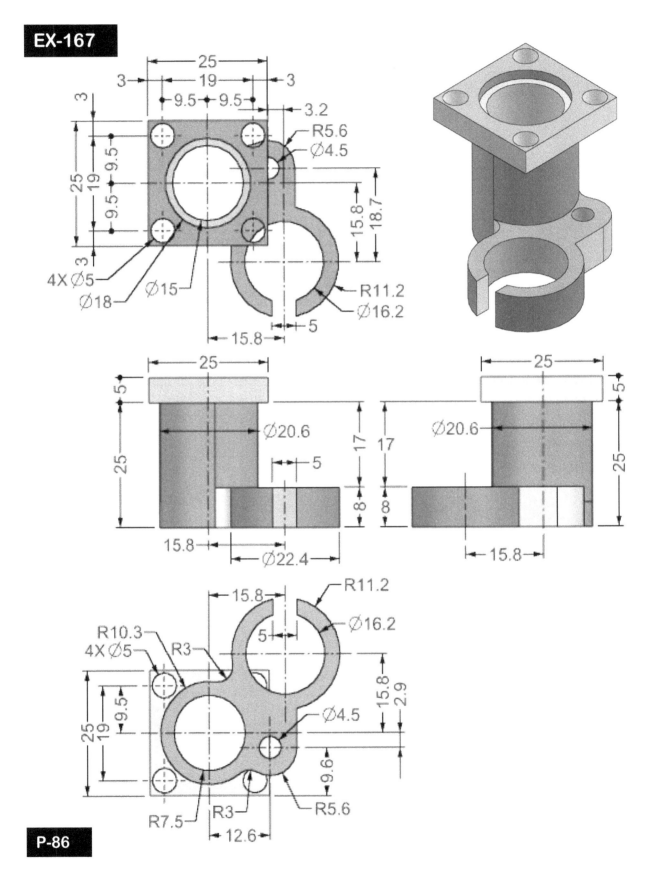

EX-167

P-86

EX-168

Ø120
PCD Ø95
8X Ø14
8X Ø10
ON PCD 95
R35
R25

A

A

6
3

32
30
80 16
32
20
2

Ø70
Ø120

30
Ø14
Ø10
16 20

Ø50
Ø70
PCD 95
Ø120

SECTION A-A

EX-169

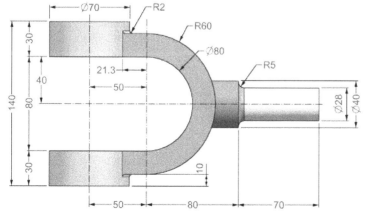

Ø70
Ø40
20
40
R5
Ø28
Ø40

50
130
70
200

Ø70
R2
R60
Ø80
R5
Ø28
Ø40

30
40
140
80
30

21.3
50
10

50
80
70

Ø70
15 40 15
10
30
80
Ø28
Ø40
15
15
70
30
10
35
Ø70

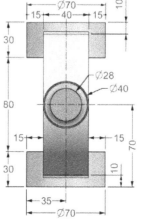

P-87

4X R2
3
2X Ø3
1
1
1
4
6
2.75 — 4.75 — Ø15 — 4.75 — 2.75
30

R7.5
R6.5
R2
13
8.5
R2
8.5
8.5
15
30
1

1
1
7.5
4
16
1
8.5
6

44
184
44
22
92
22
4X Ø23.2
R60
40
138.6
30
30
248
168
30
138.6
30
30
20
124
80
30
40
228
272

44
20
40
44
40
264
20
35
40
272

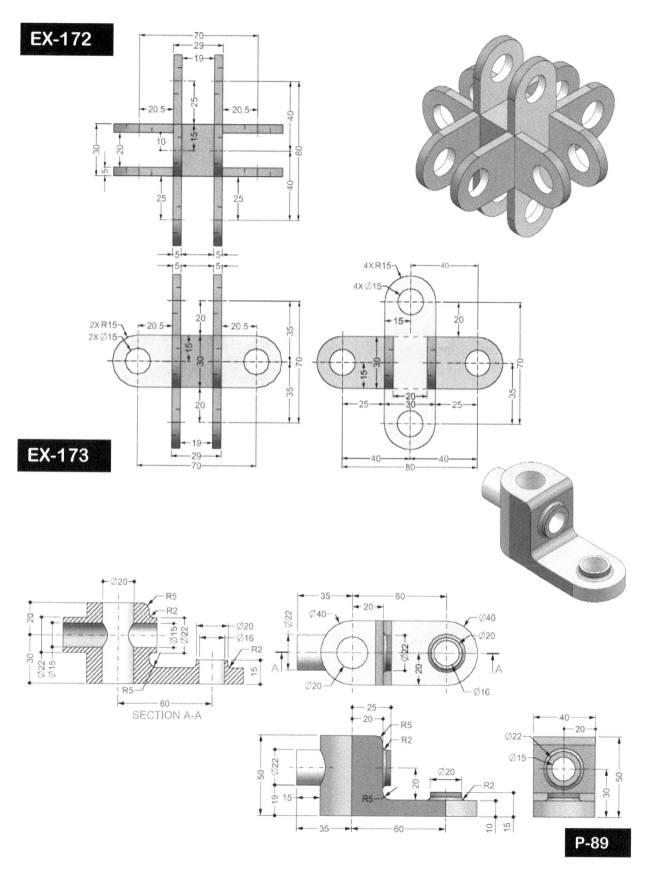

EX-172

EX-173

P-89

SECTION A-A

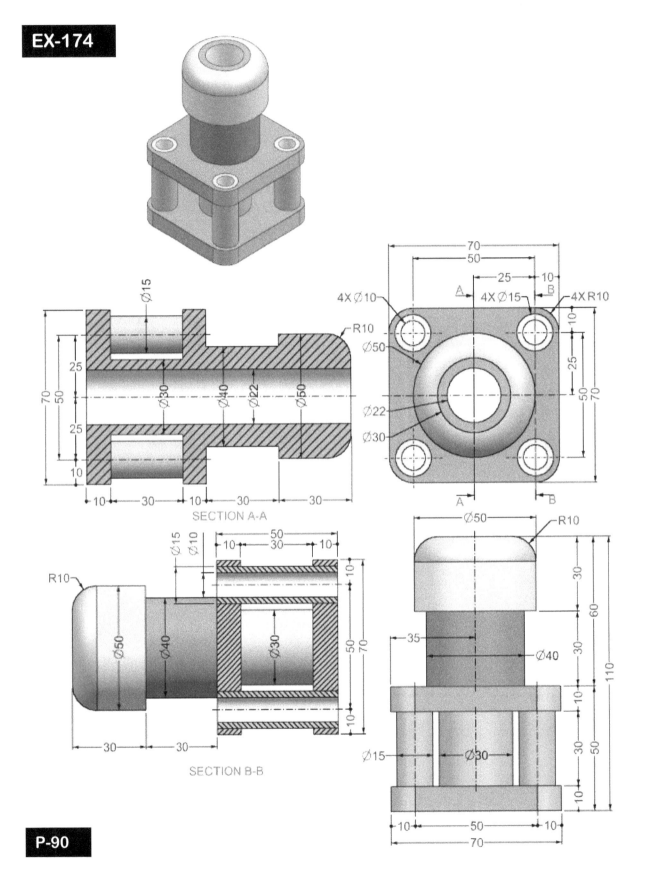

EX-174

SECTION A-A

SECTION B-B

P-90

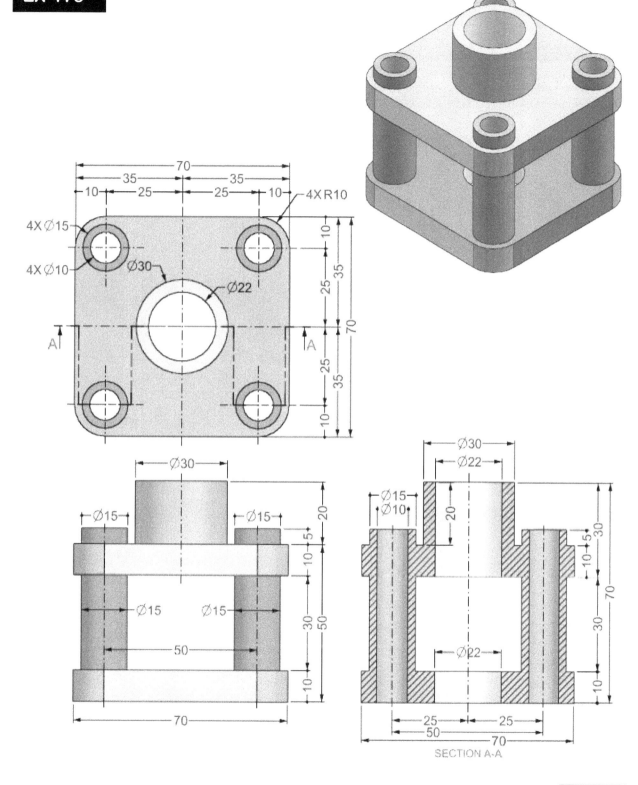

SECTION A-A

EX-176

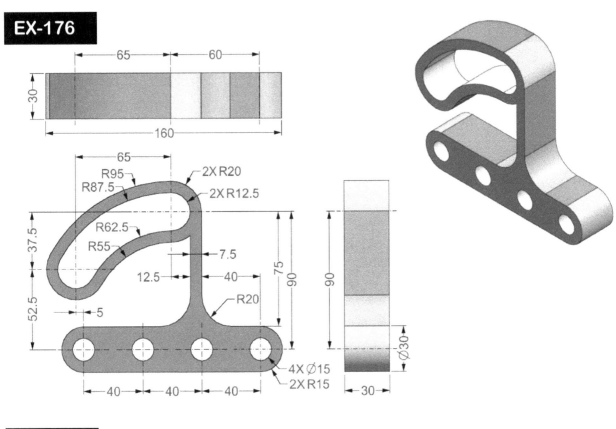

EX-177

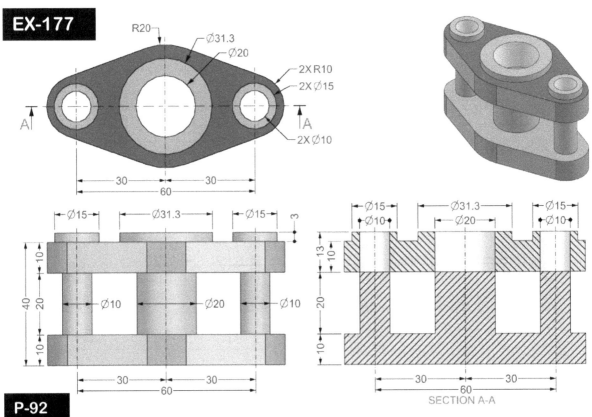

SECTION A-A

P-92

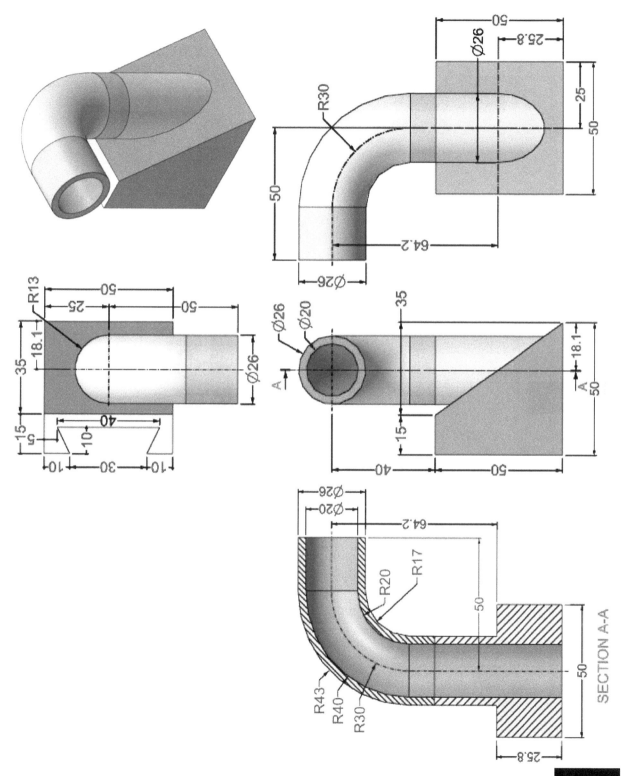

SECTION A-A

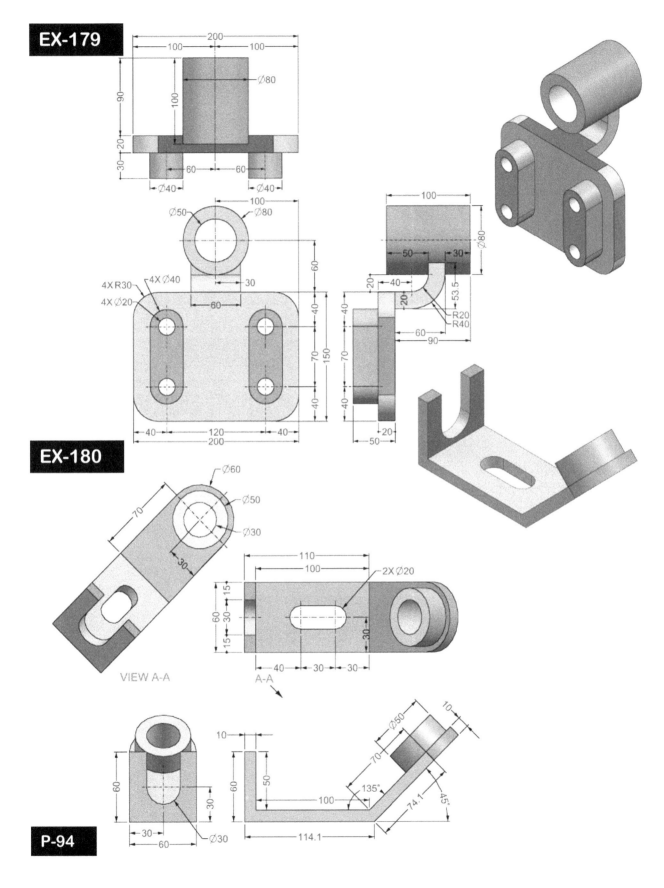

EX-179

EX-180

P-94

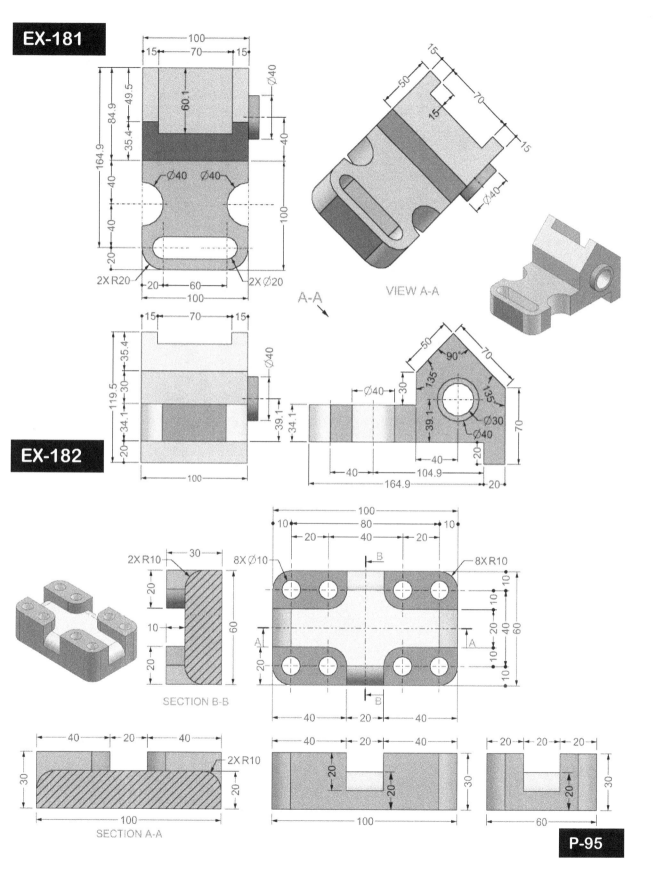

EX-181

VIEW A-A

A-A

EX-182

SECTION B-B

SECTION A-A

P-95

EX-183

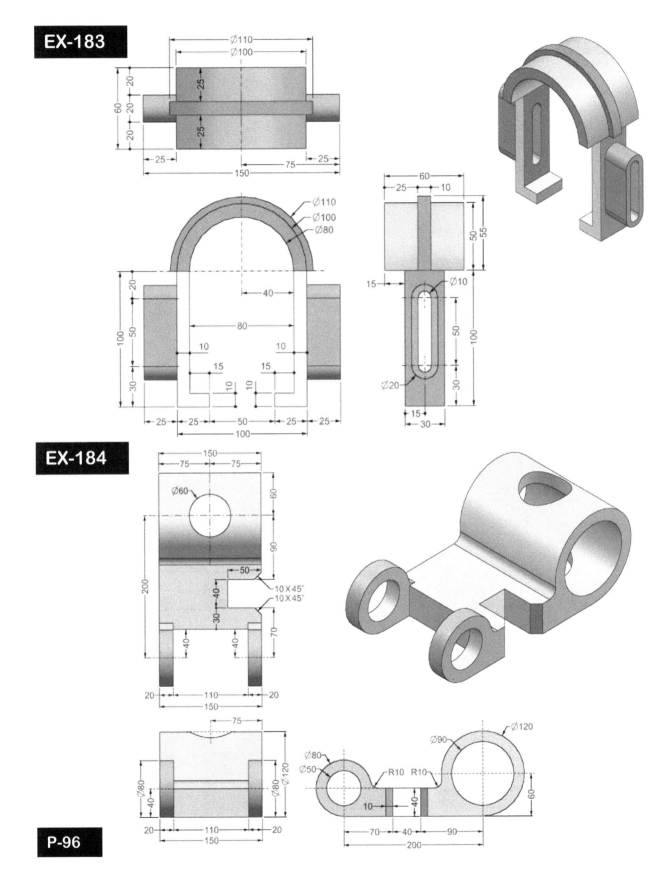

EX-184

P-96

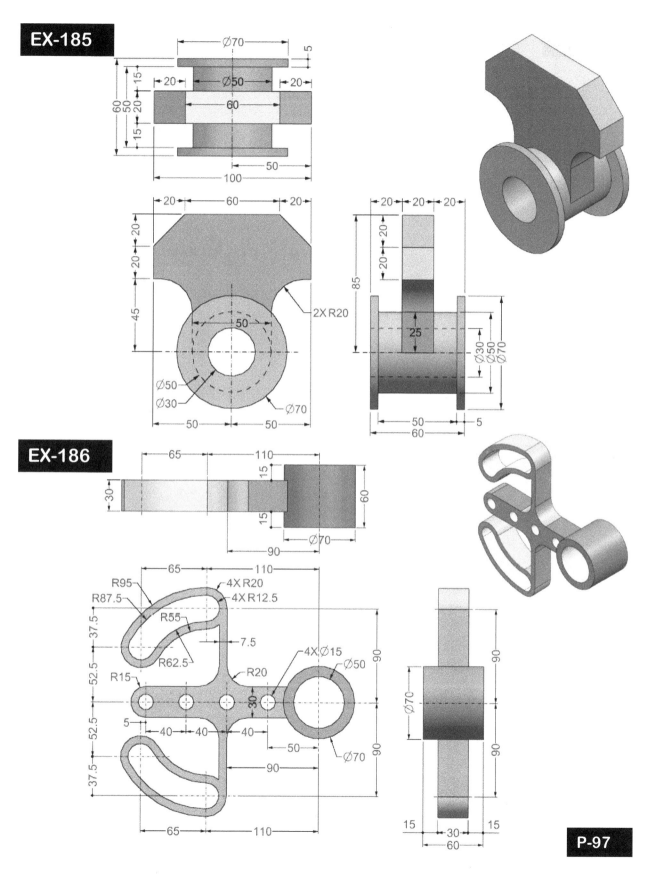

EX-185

EX-186

P-97

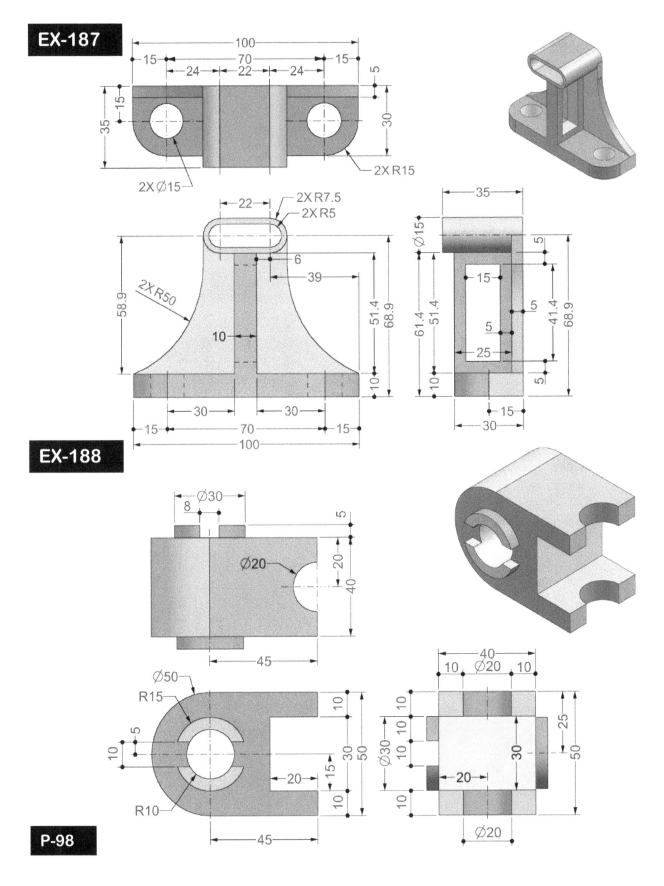

EX-187

100
15
70
15
24
22
24
5
15
35
30
2X Ø15
2X R15

22
2X R7.5
2X R5
6
39
2X R50
58.9
51.4
68.9
10
30
30
15
70
15
100

35
Ø15
5
15
61.4
51.4
5
5
68.9
41.4
10
25
5
15
30

EX-188

Ø30
8
5
Ø20
20
40
45

Ø50
R15
10
10
5
Ø30
10
50
10
30
10
15
20
10
R10
45

40
10
Ø20
10
10
25
10
Ø30
10
50
30
10
20
10
Ø20

P-98

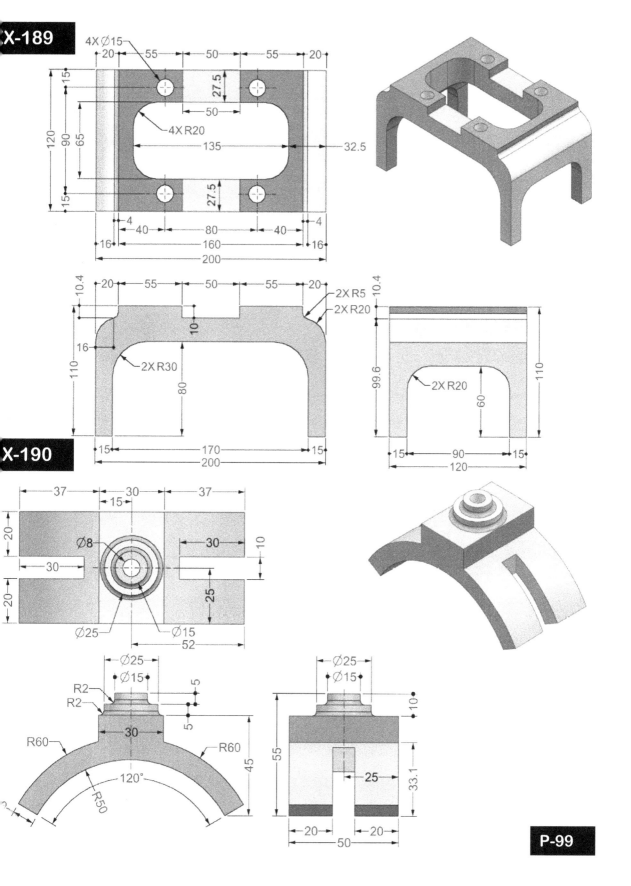

X-189

4X Ø15
20 55 50 55 20
27.5
50
4X R20
135 32.5
27.5
120 90 65
15 15
15 15
4 4
40 80 40
16 16
160
200

10.4
20 55 50 55 20
2X R5
2X R20
10
16
110
2X R30
80
15 170 15
200

10.4
2X R20
99.6
110
60
15 90 15
120

X-190

37 30 37
15
20
Ø8 30
30 10
25
20
Ø25 Ø15
52

Ø25
Ø15
R2 5
R2
30 5
R60
R60
120° 45
R50
55
25
33.1
20 20
50

P-99

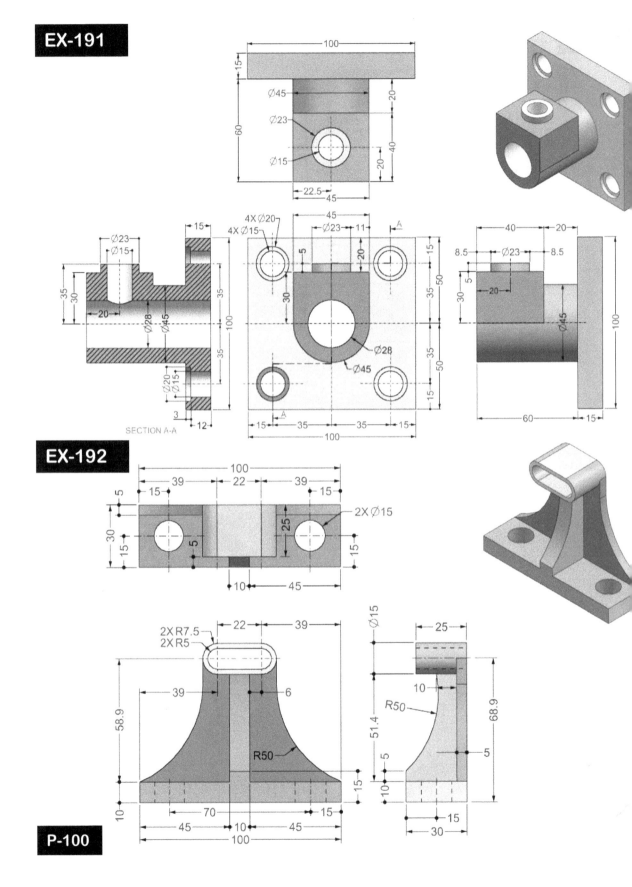

EX-191

EX-192

P-100

SECTION A-A

SECTION A-A

2X R10
2X Ø14
2X Ø8
R20
Ø30
15
30
60
30
10
Ø20
Ø30
55
A
A

40
12
10
10
80
60
10
R2
Ø20
Ø30
30
1 x 45°
Ø8
Ø14

Ø30
Ø23
R2
R2
Ø30
Ø14
40
15
10
12
55

40
Ø30
20
Ø14
R3.2
40
10
12
30
30
60

4X Ø20
150
20
110
20
55
40
20
R5
40
15
15
130
30
60
40
Ø120
30
35
40
70
40

ALL HOLES CHAMFER 2MM

130°
2X Ø20
2X Ø50
Ø120
25
75
R5
PCD Ø160
Ø100
R5
R5
40
70
40
35
20
80

60
30
15
30
80
40
30
R5
20
40
130

70
50
60
4X Ø20
20
20
110
150
BOTTOM VIEW

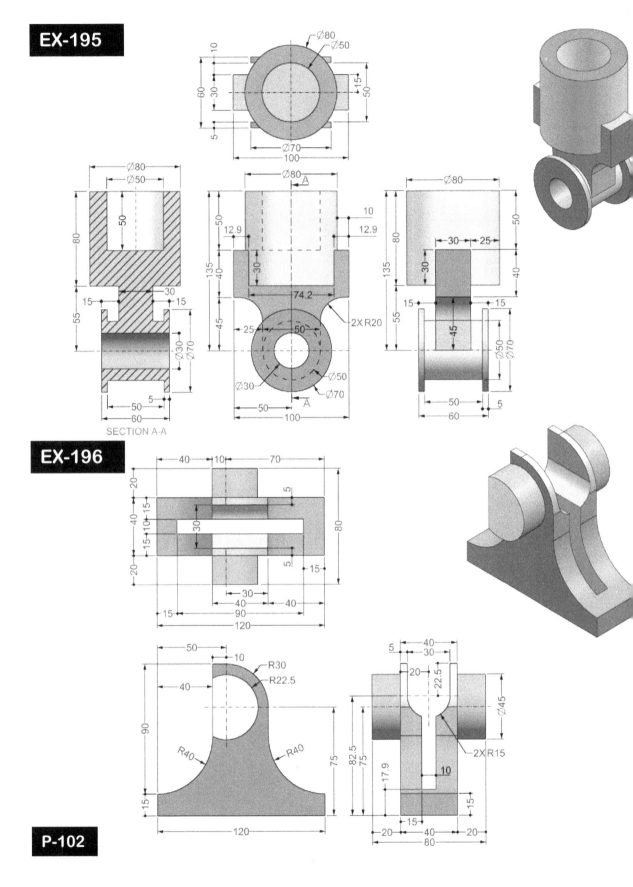

EX-195

Ø80
Ø50
10
60
30
15
50
5
Ø70
100

Ø80
Ø50
50
80
15
15
30
55
Ø30
Ø70
5
50
60
SECTION A-A

Ø80
A
50
10
135
12.9
12.9
40
30
74.2
45
25
50
2X R20
Ø50
Ø30
Ø70
50
A
100

Ø80
10
50
80
30
25
135
30
15
45
15
55
Ø50
Ø70
50
5
60

EX-196

40
10
70
20
5
40
15
10
15
30
80
15
5
20
15
30
15
40
40
90
120

50
10
R30
R22.5
40
R40
R40
90
75
15
120

5
40
30
20
22.5
Ø45
82.5
75
2X R15
17.9
10
15
15
20
40
20
80

P-102

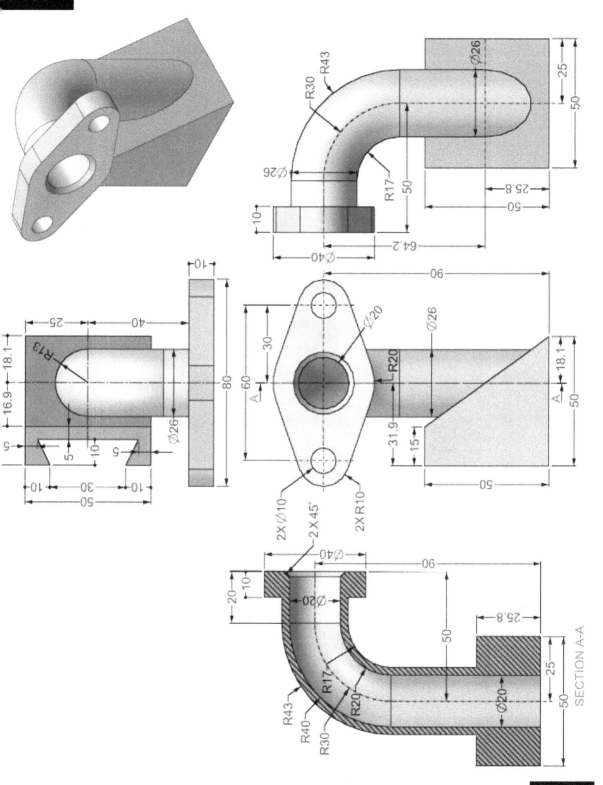

SECTION A-A

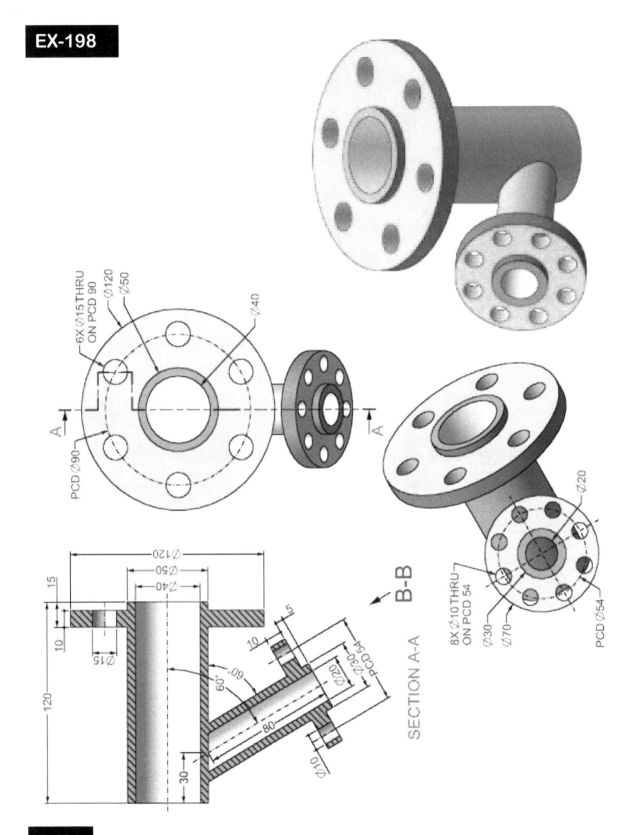

6X Ø15 THRU ON PCD 90
Ø120
Ø50
Ø40
PCD Ø90
A
A

Ø20
8X Ø10 THRU ON PCD 54
Ø30
Ø70
PCD Ø54

Ø120
Ø50
Ø40
15
10
Ø15
120
60°
60°
80
30
Ø10
5
10
Ø20
Ø30
PCD 54
B-B
SECTION A-A

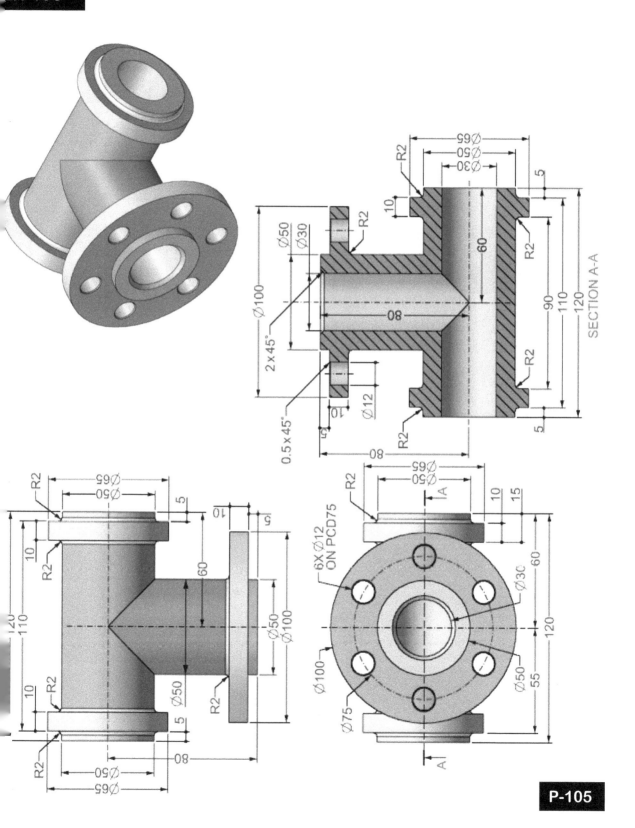

SECTION A-A

Ø65
Ø50
Ø30
5
10
60
90
110
120
R2
R2
R2
R2
Ø100
Ø50
Ø30
R2
R2
2×45°
0.5×45°
10
Ø12
08
80

Ø65
Ø50
5
10
5
R2
R2
10
R2
60
120
110
10
R2
R2
Ø50
Ø100
R2
5
80
Ø50
Ø65

Ø65
Ø50
A
10
15
R2
6X Ø12
ON PCD75
Ø30
60
120
55
Ø50
Ø100
Ø75
A

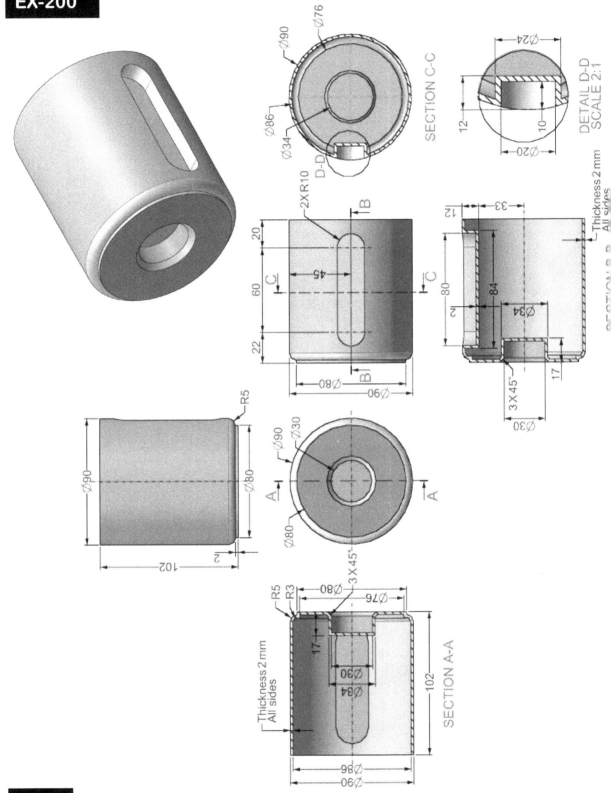

SECTION C-C

DETAIL D-D
SCALE 2:1

Thickness 2 mm
All sides

2X R10

SECTION A-A

R5

Thickness 2 mm
All sides

3 X 45°

Other useful books by CADIN360

1. 150 CAD Exercises

2. AutoCAD Exercises

3. CAD Exercises

4. 50+ SolidWorks Exercises

5. SolidWorks 200 Exercises

6. Autodesk Inventor Exercises

7. Catia Exercises

8. Siemens NX Exercises

www.ingramcontent.com/pod-product-compliance
Lightning Source LLC
Chambersburg PA
CBHW080431060326
40689CB00019B/4460